CW00746435

BONKERS
BOOKS

WEE on a JELLYFISH STING

and OTHER LIES that grown-ups tell YOU

RITTEN by

Tracey Turner

Illustrated by **Clive Goddard**

■SCHOLASTIC

Scholastic Children's Books,
Euston House, 24 Eversholt Street,
London, NW1 1DB, UK

A division of Scholastic Ltd
London ~ New York ~ Toronto ~ Sydney ~ Auckland
Mexico City ~ New Delhi ~ Hong Kong

First published in the UK by Scholastic Ltd, 2010

Text copyright © Tracey Turner, 2010
Illustration copyright © Clive Goddard, 2010
All rights reserved

ISBN 978 1407 11650 1

Printed and bound in the UK by CPI Mackays, Chatham ME5 8TD

2 4 6 8 10 9 7 5 3 1

The right of Tracey Turner and Clive Goddard to be identified as the author and illustrator
of this work has been asserted by them in accordance with the Copyright, Designs and
Patents Act, 1988.

This book is sold subject to the condition that it shall not, by way of trade or otherwise
be lent, resold, hired out, or otherwise circulated without the publisher's prior consent in
any form of binding or cover other than that in which it is published and without a
similar condition, including this condition, being imposed on a subsequent purchaser.

ALL of the old RUBBISH spouted by adults could fill several **thick** BOOKS

→ INTRODUCTION

As you probably already know, grown-ups talk an awful lot of nonsense. In fact all of the old rubbish spouted by adults could fill several thick books. This one is a start, at least, on the road to exposing and explaining the **whopping great porkers** they tell.

Some adults may not realize that some (or all) of what they're saying is complete twaddle – perhaps they read it on the internet and so assume it must be true. Others will gladly tell great big fibs in order to get you to stop doing something, start doing something, or leave them alone. Whatever their reasons for talking rubbish, now is your chance to shut them up for good.

Read on and find out ...

☞ **The truth about bread crusts, falling coconuts and head lice**

☞ **What really happens when you chop a worm in half**

☞ **Whether Napoleon was short or Columbus discovered America**

... as well as hundreds of fascinating facts. With any luck, and your patient explanations, the grown-ups in your life might eventually stop spouting drivel.

Animals 🐥

Butterflies EMERGE from cocoons

Most adults – even teachers – are convinced of this, but they are completely wrong. Sigh heavily and explain the facts ...

Moths and butterflies start off as a tiny egg. Caterpillars hatch from the eggs and eat leaves for the next few weeks. Then the caterpillars of both moths and butterflies go through a similar stage: they attach themselves to a plant, form an outer covering, and transform themselves into a butterfly or moth over a period of weeks or months. The creature is a pupa during this stage, also known as a chrysalis in the case of butterflies. But only moths make a cocoon – a hard outer casing to protect the pupa. The chrysalis of a butterfly is not encased in a cocoon at all, no matter what many adults, or *The Very Hungry Caterpillar*, might tell you.

it's TRUE!

The fluids inside the N'gwa caterpillar, found in Africa, are highly poisonous. Hunters use them to poison the tips of their arrows.

GEOGRAPHY

Quicksand sucks you down into a BOTTOMLESS pit

It's amazing how many grown-ups take their 'general knowledge' from old films, which sometimes feature deadly pits of quicksand sucking helpless victims to a horrible fate.

In fact, quicksand is just very wet sand, or silt, most often caused by an underground spring. It can be deceptive because it might look almost the same as the ground around it. But it doesn't suck things into it, it won't drag you down to the bottom, and if you fall into a patch of quicksand by accident you can probably just

walk to the side and step out. (Far from being 'bottomless', quicksand is usually quite shallow.) If the quicksand is too deep to stand up in, a person can easily swim to the side. In fact, it's easier to float in quicksand than in clear water. So, if you ever encounter quicksand on your intrepid travels, don't panic. And if anyone tries to warn you about pits of quicksand that will suck you down to your doom, simply laugh bravely and soldier on – with arm bands if necessary.

TOP TIPS FOR ESCAPING FROM QUICKSAND

* Don't panic.

* Take off back pack if wearing one. Also remove bricks or other heavy objects from pockets.

* Walk to edge of quicksand. Or ...

* Float to edge of quicksand.

* Dry off.

HISTORY 📖

The DRUIDS built Stonehenge

Stonehenge stands on Salisbury Plain in Wiltshire, England. It's one of the world's most famous prehistoric monuments, yet some adults are very badly informed about it. If anyone comes out with this piece of nonsense, try asking them who the Druids were, when they lived, and when and how they built Stonehenge. The results will be hilarious.

Stonehenge was first built out of earth around 5,000 years ago, during Britain's Neolithic period (or the New Stone Age). Less than a hundred years later, a wooden structure was built. Around 4,500 years ago, the first stones were brought to the site. During the centuries that followed, more stones were brought and the site was rearranged. The final changes to the monument were made about 3,600 years ago, during Britain's Bronze Age. After that, it fell into ruin. No one knows what it was used for: guesses include a temple, an observatory, or an alien spacecraft landing pad (some guesses are a little eccentric). The Druids were Celtic priests who lived about 1,000 years after Stonehenge had been abandoned, and they had absolutely nothing to do with building it.

The confusion about Druids came about because of two men who studied Stonehenge during the 1600s and 1700s, John Aubrey and William Stukeley. Both correctly guessed that Stonehenge was prehistoric. Since the Druids were some of the only prehistoric people that anyone knew about at the time, Aubrey started the belief that the monument was built by Druids. William Stukeley agreed and became very enthusiastic about them - he even dressed as a Druid. By the end of the 18th century there was a secret society called the Ancient Order of Druids, with its own secret passwords, special robes and even druidical haircuts. Modern-day Druids continue to visit Stonehenge, despite the fact that there is no evidence to suggest that Celtic Druids had anything to do with the place at all.

it's TRUE!

There are two sorts of stones at Stonehenge: the smaller ones, known as bluestones, weigh about the same as two rhinos; the bigger ones, the sarsen stones, weigh as much as four African elephants. The sarsen stones were brought to Stonehenge from about 30 km away, and the bluestones came all the way from Wales – in a time before there was any wheeled transport at all.

HUMAN BODY

Head LICE prefer clean hair

If you've ever had head lice, some well-meaning adult might have told you something along these lines. Maybe they believed it, or maybe they said it just to make you feel better. Either way, it isn't true.

Head lice are tiny brownish-coloured insects that feed on blood on the human scalp. They are passed from person to person by contact (only people get them, not animals), and anyone with hair can get them. They don't prefer clean hair, dirty hair, straight, curly, dark or blonde hair: they are not at all fussy. You're more likely to catch them if you have long hair, though, because there's more chance of your hair coming into contact with someone else's. They're common among children because groups of children are much more likely to touch heads than adults are. The lice can't jump or fly. They spend their whole lives – which last about a month – on a human head, laying their eggs glued to the base of the hair (these are white and known as 'nits'). They're not a sign of poor hygiene, but neither are they a sign that the creatures have 'chosen' someone's hair because it is clean.

it's TRUE!

You're almost certain to have parasites called demodex mites living in your eyelashes and eyebrows. They are unlikely to do you any harm, and you won't know they're there.

They don't prefer clean hair, **dirty hair**, STRAIGHT, curly, dark or **blonde hair**: they are not at all fussy.

Animals

An AARDVAARK is a type of anteater

Lots of adults think aardvaarks are a type of anteater. While it's true that aardvaarks eat termites (which are insects that look like ants, but aren't), they are not related to anteaters. In fact, they don't exist on the same continent.

Aardvaarks live in Africa, where they spend their lives terrorizing termites. They use their powerful claws to break into termite mounds, and their long, sticky tongues to eat as many as possible. Their large ears alert them to termite activity. Despite the similarity of their long snouts to anteaters', aardvaarks evolved completely separately. In fact, they have no other relatives that still exist. Anteaters live in South America, eat ants and termites, and are related to sloths.

An aardvaark can eat half a million termites in one meal.

14

HISTORY 📖

Christopher COLUMBUS discovered America

Columbus Day is celebrated with a day off for everyone in the United States. There's even a rhyme about Christopher Columbus ('In fourteen hundred and ninety two / Columbus sailed the ocean blue...'). So it might come as news to some adults that Christopher Columbus didn't discover America at all.

First of all, of course, America had already been 'discovered', by the people who had been living there for centuries. Here your grown-up will probably protest, 'yes, but I meant the first non-native American to travel there.' Columbus wasn't even the first to do that – the Vikings had landed in North America centuries before Columbus, and there are also claims of Irish, African, Polynesian and Chinese voyages (among others) to the North American mainland before Columbus got there.

Christopher Columbus sailed to one of the islands now called the Bahamas. He stopped off at Cuba and a few other places but never set foot on the North American mainland. He thought the islands were off the coast of India (which

15

is why they're known today as the West Indies) and carried on thinking he'd landed in Asia, rather than a completely different continent, until he died in 1506. So, one way or another, it's fair to say that America wasn't discovered by Christopher Columbus.

it's TRUE!

You might have noticed that America is called America and not Columbia. One theory is that the continent was named after explorer Amerigo Vespucci, who travelled to South America around 1500. Another theory suggests it was named after Amerrique, a gold-mining district of Nicaragua. There are other theories too – no one is entirely sure which one is correct.

FOOD AND DRINK 🥣

Tapping a can of FIZZY drink stops it from foaming when you open it

Have you ever noticed an adult seriously and intently tapping the top or side of a can of fizzy drink with a finger? If you ask them what they're doing they are almost certain to say that the tapping will stop the can from foaming when they open it. Now is your chance to tell them that they are talking nonsense.

Fizzy drinks owe their fizz to carbon dioxide dissolved under pressure in the liquid. When the can is unopened, there are no bubbles inside the can because of pressure. When you open the can, the pressure is reduced and bubbles form and rise to the surface. If the can has been given a good shake, bubbles are created inside the can and these will be waiting to burst out in a shower of foam when it's opened. There's nothing you can do to avoid this, other than waiting a while before you open the can.

If your adult is especially stubborn, he or she might try and tell you that the tapping dislodges the bubbles formed by shaking from the sides and bottom of the can and makes

17

them collect in the air pocket at the top, so they will not cause so much foam. But if you are tapping the can hard enough to dislodge bubbles from the sides, you only risk forming new ones.

Try it yourself...

... and find out it doesn't work! Conduct an experiment:

* Shake two fizzy drinks cans the same number of times and with equal force

* Tap one on the side ten times with your forefinger

* Open both cans

* Do a lot of wiping up

* Change your clothes

* Log your results

SPACE

There are nine PLANETS in the solar system

Any adult who believes this is woefully out of date.

There are eight planets in our solar system. Starting with the closest planet to the Sun, they are: Mercury, Venus, Earth, Mars, Jupiter, Saturn, Uranus and Neptune. Until 2006 there was a ninth planet, Pluto. But in that year, the International Astronomical Union decided that Pluto didn't meet its definition of a planet, and demoted it to the status of 'dwarf planet'. Pluto is about 20% of the size of Earth's moon.

it's TRUE! Ceres, the largest asteroid in the asteroid belt, was considered a planet for about 50 years after its discovery. In 1850, it was demoted from a planet to an asteroid. It's now known as a dwarf planet, like Pluto.

SOLAR SYSTEM

HISTORY 📖

Ferdinand Magellan was the first person to circumnavigate the WORLD

A grown-up might tell you this in a clever-sounding voice (probably quite pleased with the word 'circumnavigate'), but they're wrong. Magellan was the person who started off leading the first round-the-world expedition, but he ended up too dead to be the first person to circumnavigate the world.

In 1519 Ferdinand Magellan set off from Spain, with five ships and about 260 men. He was aiming to sail right around the world, which had never been done before. Three years

later, one of the ships arrived back in Spain, having completed a round-the-world trip. There were just 18 surviving men on board, and Magellan wasn't one of them. He'd been killed about halfway round, fighting against Philippine islanders. When the expedition arrived back in Spain it was led by Juan Sebastien Elcano, who became the first person to sail around the world in a single trip (along with the other 17 men, who don't get a mention in history books at all).

it's TRUE!

The circumference of the Earth at the Equator is about 40,000 km. The voyage completed by Elcano and his crew was reported as 14,460 leagues – depending on which definition of a league you use, this is somewhere between 70,000 and 80,000 km.

Animals

Camels carry water in their HUMPS

Camels can last for a long time without having a drink, which is very handy in the desert. But if you've ever been told by an adult that this is because camels store water in their humps, you've listened to yet more grown-up rubbish.

Camels' humps sometimes look fairly rigid and sometimes floppy, which may be the reason some people think they carry water. In fact, the humps store fat, so if they're looking droopy it means the animals haven't had much to eat recently. Camels are well adapted to life in a dry climate and

STILL OR SPARKLING?

have various ways of conserving water: they hardly sweat, they recycle the moisture in their breath, and they don't lose water by panting or in their dung, which is dry enough to burn even when it's fresh.

It's TRUE!

Bactrian (or Asian) camels have two humps, and dromedaries (or Arabian camels) have one. The animals were imported into Australia from the Middle East during the 1800s and now Australia has the world's only herds of wild camels.

24

HISTORY 📖

Napoleon was VERY short

Some shorter men are sometimes accused of having a 'Napoleon complex', which means they strut around being bossy in order to make up for not being very tall. But – wrong again, adults – Napoleon wasn't really shorter than average at all.

Napoleon, French Emperor from 1804, measured five feet two inches, which is rather short for a man. But he was five feet two in French feet and inches, which are different from British ones (in the days before metric weights and measures, everything was a lot more complicated). In British feet and inches Napoleon would have been five feet six inches, about average for a French man in the 1800s, when people used to be a bit shorter than they are today.

Apart from the confusing French and British measurements, people might have assumed Napoleon was a short man because he was known as 'le petit corporal' ('the little corporal'). 'Petit' is the French word for 'little' but it's also used as a term of endearment. Napoleon wasn't a corporal either; he was a top ranking general. French people called him 'le petit corporal' to show that he'd muck in with his men instead of just strutting about barking orders (though he must have done a fair bit of that). Also, Napoleon's guards were made up of the tallest men in the country, and next to them Napoleon looked short, even though he wasn't really.

You can tell your ill-informed adult that Napoleon wasn't short. His English enemies probably liked to think he was: Napoleon was a great military leader with a huge army and plans to invade England, so it might have helped to think of him as a little pipsqueak.

it's TRUE!

In 2005, one of Napoleon's teeth was auctioned in England. Someone paid £11,000 for it.

HEALTH 👁

Cracking your KNUCKLES gives you arthritis

It's true that the sound of cracking knuckles isn't the nicest sound in the world, but do adults really have to tell lies in order to stop you from doing it?

When you crack your knuckles you're pulling or pushing the joints in your fingers out of their normal position. Joints are the meeting points of two bones and there's a special fluid that surrounds them, called synovial fluid. The synovial fluid is full of dissolved gases, which form bubbles and escape when the joint is pulled, causing the popping sound. There's no evidence at all to suggest that this could cause arthritis.*

Still, pulling your joints all the time can't be a good idea, and it can cause a slight decrease in grip. And that sound is pretty horrible...

*Painful inflamation of the joints.

It's TRUE!

✸On average there are 206 bones in the human body. The number can vary from person to person – you might have as few as 200 or as many as 210. Babies have more – over 300 – but the bones fuse together as they grow.

✸The longest bone in the human body is the femur, or thigh bone.

✸The smallest bone is the stapes, or stirrup, in the middle ear.

HISTORY 📖

SAINT Patrick was Irish

Another thing grown-ups get wrong, although you might be generous and forgive them for doing so.

Saint Patrick was born in the fourth century AD. No one knows where for certain – probably Scotland or England. But he certainly wasn't born in Ireland. Saint Patrick was kidnapped from the west of England or Scotland by Irish raiders when he was in his teens and spent six years in Ireland as a slave to a chieftain, who set him to work herding animals. Eventually Patrick escaped. He became a priest and later returned to Ireland to spread Christianity. The Irish forgave him for being English or Scottish and made him their patron saint. Today, many people celebrate Saint Patrick's Day confident that Patrick was Irish – until you put them right.

SAINTLY FACTS:

Saints change with the times: in 1958, Saint Clare of Assisi was made the patron saint of television. In 2006, Saint Isadore of Seville was made the patron saint of the Internet.

Marconi INVENTED radio

You'd think some adults weren't paying any attention in school at all, wouldn't you?

Heinrich Hertz made the first radio transmission in 1887. Marconi has become famous as the inventor of radio because he improved Hertz' invention so that it could be put to practical use. Until Marconi, radio signals couldn't be transmitted for long distances, which isn't much use at all – in fact Hertz's radio signal only crossed the width of a room. In 1901, Marconi transmitted a radio signal across the Atlantic Ocean, which is quite a bit more impressive (and about 3,500 kilometres further).

Radio solved its first MURDER case in 1910

it's TRUE!

✳ Radio solved its first murder case in 1910. Dr Crippen, who had murdered his wife in London, was on board a ship crossing the Atlantic bound for Canada. The captain of the ship thought he recognized Crippen and used the Marconi radio equipment to contact the detective on the murder case in London, who took a faster ship and arrested Crippen as he disembarked.

✳ In 1912, the first voyage of the TITANIC came to a terrible end when it hit an iceberg in the Atlantic. Radio communication alerted another ship, which changed its course and rescued survivors from the icy sea.

ANIMALS 🐤

Lemmings commit mass suicide by LEAPING over cliffs

Lemmings are small rodents, a bit like hamsters, that live in colder climates. If you ask an adult about them, they might tell you that the creatures are famous for leaping over cliffs and deliberately killing themselves. But this is another example of grown-up nonsense.

Lemmings can reproduce very quickly and this sometimes leads to an awful lot of lemmings – too many for their habitat to support. So the lemmings go in search of new areas to populate, and because of this many of the rodents get squished by cars, or even fall over cliffs. For many years people believed that the lemmings were committing suicide in a selfless bid to reduce the lemming population. A Disney film called WHITE WILDERNESS, made in the 1950s, showed lemmings jumping off a cliff and claimed that they were committing suicide. The film was faked – the lemmings were chucked into a river in Canada by members of the film crew – and helped to keep the myth alive.

it's TRUE!

The world's biggest rodents are capybaras, native to South America. They grow to about 1.3 metres long and weigh around 65 kg. They look rather like huge, long-legged guinea pigs, which are their close relatives.

PLACES 🌐

The Great Wall of China is the only MAN-MADE object visible from space

Adults will tell you this without having any real idea of what they are talking about. Alternatively, they might say that the Great Wall is the only man-made object visible from the Moon. Ask them how far away 'space' is. And how come the Great Wall can be seen while the NASA Vehicle Assembly Building can't, even though the NASA building is bigger? They will probably want to change the subject.

According to the Fédération Aéronautique Internationale, space starts 100 km above the surface of the Earth. From that height, the Great Wall of China is visible, along with lots of other man-made things. The Great Wall is only about 10 meters across so there's no reason that it should be visible while other, bigger objects aren't. From the Moon, 400,000 km away, no man-made objects can be seen at all.

The story about the Great Wall got started after it was mentioned in a book published in 1938 – before anyone had been into space at all. Even now, many grown-ups will happily repeat it, until you *stop* them.

it's TRUE!

✷ The Great Wall of China was built during the Ming Dynasty (1368-1644) but earlier walls had been built to keep out northern invaders from 2,600 years ago. The current wall stretches for 7,300 km altogether (including its various branches).

✷ The board game Trivial Pursuit included an incorrect question about the only man-made object visible from the Moon, which it claimed was the Great Wall of China.

Bonkers! ◎

You should apply BUTTER to burned skin

Really, some adults are a danger to themselves and others. No matter how forcefully they tell you that putting butter on a burn is a good idea, don't do it. They're bonkers.

In the past, people believed that butter formed a protective layer and the burn could heal underneath it. Unfortunately, butter – especially warm butter that people have been slapping on their skin – can easily become a breeding ground for harmful bacteria. Anyone following this old-fashioned advice could end up in hospital because of a minor burn. The best thing to do if you burn yourself is to soak the burn in cool water, then apply an antiseptic cream. If the burn's serious you need to get medical attention quickly.

DON'T do it.
They're BONKERS

36

CRAZY CURES

* A Saxon cure for warts: Take a piece of meat, rub it on the wart then bury it. As the meat rots away, the wart will disappear.

* A nineteenth-century cure for a chest infection: drink tea made from snails.

* An ancient Roman cure for toothache: strap a toad to the jaw.

* A medieval cure for rheumatism: carry a dead shrew in your pocket.

* A nineteenth-century cure for whooping cough: swallow a spider covered in butter.

ANIMALS 🐔

The cheetah is the world's FASTEST animal

Grown-ups are wrong about this by about 208 km/h.

Cheetahs are the fastest land animal, belting along at 112 km/h. But the peregrine falcon has been recorded at speeds of 320 km/h as it dives down to catch its prey. If you think diving is cheating, another bird, the white-throated spine-tail swift, is still a lot faster than a cheetah as it flies along in the more usual, horizontal plane – it reaches speeds of 177 km/h.

spine-tail swift: A LOT **FASTER** THAN A **CHEETAH**

BIRD

peregrine falcon - 320 km/h

LAND ANIMAL

cheetah - 112 km/h

FISH

sailfish - 109 km/h

BIRD ON LAND

ostrich - 72 km/h

INSECT

dragonfly - 57 km/h

PLACES

The SAHARA is the largest desert on earth

Some grown-ups obviously didn't pay very much attention in geography lessons. Deserts don't have to be hot and sandy.

A desert is a place where there is less than 25 cm² of rainfall per year, so cold places can be deserts as well as hot ones. The largest desert on earth is Antarctica, which is also the coldest place on earth. Antarctica covers an area of around 14 million km², and if it was a country (it isn't, it's a continent) it would be the second biggest in the world, after Russia. The Arctic, another polar desert, is the world's second largest desert. The Sahara desert gets third place: it's almost as big as the United States of America (it's around 9 million km²), and it's the largest hot desert in the world. So you could be generous and tell your adult that they are almost right.

it's TRUE!

* Antarctica shivers underneath 90% of the world's ice.

* In the Dry Valleys of Antarctica it hasn't rained for millions of years.

* The coldest natural temperature on Earth was recorded in Antarctica at the Russian base Vostok - it was -89.4 °C.

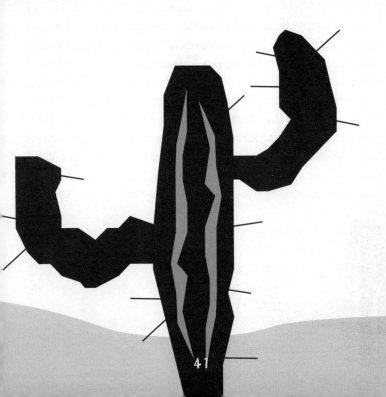

HISTORY 📖

Walter Raleigh introduced POTATOES and tobacco to Britain

There used to be a lot of fair old nonsense taught in history lessons, and adults today are the result. Now is your chance to stop the spread of rubbish any further.

To be fair, lots of people make the tobacco-potato-Raleigh connection, possibly because he was an Elizabethan celebrity and people liked to talk about him and copy him, so he was credited with all sorts of things. Tobacco arrived in Britain from France, not directly from the New World, (as America was known in the 1500s) where it comes from originally. Snuff-taking and smoking became popular in England soon after they did in France, and Walter Raleigh himself was fond of smoking, even though he can't be held responsible for introducing it.

Potatoes originally come from the New World too. Although Raleigh travelled there, he didn't bring back the first potatoes. They had arrived in Europe before he was born, brought by the Spanish from their new-found territories, and quickly spread throughout the rest of Europe.

★ Jean Nicot was the French diplomat who introduced the tobacco plant to France. Ironically, he championed it because of its health-giving properties. Nicotine is named after him.

★ Walter Raleigh didn't remain popular in the Elizabethan court. In 1618 he was executed for treason. Raleigh's body was buried but his wife kept his head in a leather bag until she died in 1647. The head passed to his son – when he died – the head was finally buried with him.

POTATOES arrived in **Europe** before Raleigh was born

BONKERS! ◎

Eating bread crusts makes your hair CURLY

Some of the lies told by grown-ups are plainly ridiculous, and this is one of them. But such is the adult desire to see you eat everything on your plate they will tell you almost anything. If your hair is curly anyway, or if you're happy not to have curly hair, adults may try telling you that crusts increase your height or general levels of attractiveness. At last, here is your chance to find out the truth about bread crusts and their true powers.

As you probably already know, curly hair is down to your genetic make-up and has nothing to do with bread crusts or any other food you eat. If you want curly hair, use tongs or get a perm (although you could well be committing a grave fashion error).

However, research has shown that bread crusts contain more of a particular antioxidant, formed in the baking process, than the rest of the bread. Antioxidants are most commonly found in fruit and vegetables (Vitamin C is an antioxidant) and they're believed to help prevent cell damage. So it turns out that eating your crusts might be good for you after all.

Generally speaking, darker-coloured breads have more antioxidant than lighter-coloured ones.

it's TRUE!

There are about 100,000 hairs on the average human head, though if you're a redhead you'll probably have fewer, and if your hair is blonde you're likely to have more.

CURLY HAIR IS DOWN TO YOUR GENETIC MAKE-UP

SCIENCE

Lightning never STRIKES twice in the same place

Grown-ups sometimes use this expression to mean that the same piece of bad luck is unlikely to happen twice to the same person. But it's amazing how many of them believe it's literally true.

Lightning is caused by electrically charged water droplets at the bottom of clouds. Sometimes they are close enough to the Earth to be attracted to it, and electrical energy is released in a flash of lightning (occasionally lightning can come from the top of clouds). Tall buildings or trees or even people all make easier conductors to the Earth than the air does, and that's why they are sometimes struck by lightning.

Being struck by lightning once does not mean it won't happen again. In fact, since the object attracted the lightning in the first place, lightning is more likely to be strike in the same place again than in other places in the same vicinity. Tall buildings are often struck twice during the same thunderstorm. The Sears Tower in Chicago was recently recorded being struck by lightning twice in the space of five minutes: the building is struck between 40 and 90 times a year.

★ The spark from a flash of lightning can measure eight kilometres long.

★ You're not necessarily safe during a thunderstorm even if you're indoors: people have been injured while talking on a landline phone because the electrical charge can travel down the phone line.

ANIMALS

Goldfish have a THREE-SECOND memory

Perhaps adults tell you this just to make you feel better about our scaly friends, or perhaps they think it's true. It isn't.

Research has shown that goldfish can remember things for several months. They can be trained to operate a lever in return for food and can learn that there are particular times of day when the lever works and doesn't work. Goldfish pets have been taught tricks, such as zigzagging through poles and pushing a ball through a hoop. Maybe it's time to get Goldie a bigger bowl?

FISHY FACTS

✶ Some fish can survive on land for short periods of time. The spotted climbing perch can absorb oxygen from the air and can pull itself along the ground on its strong pectoral fins.

✶ The world's largest fish is the whale shark, which can measure up to 12.5 metres long.

✶ The world's smallest fish is a tiny member of the carp family, measured at less than 8 mm long.

Try it yourself

... and find out your goldfish is a lot cleverer than you thought.

✶ If you feed your fish twice a day, use feeding times for 15-minute training sessions.

✶ Start with something simple like swimming through a hoop. Every time your fish swims through the hoop, reward it with a small amount of food.

✶ Within two weeks your fish will be able to perform at least one trick. Try getting your fish to swim through a tube, under a pole (goldfish limbo), or even push a football into a goal.

BONKERS!

If you swallow a melon seed or cherry stone, a plant will start to GROW in your stomach

Have you heard a grown-up come out with this old twaddle? Presumably it's because they think eating seeds or stones is bad for you. (It's not — though eating a big stone could be dangerous.) It's a mystery why they think it's going to be effective, though. As long as you're over three years old you're very unlikely to believe it.

it's TRUE! The world's biggest seed is a type of coconut known as the coco de mer. It can weigh up to 20 kilograms.

HISTORY 📖

George Washington was the first American PRESIDENT

If an adult tells you this, you might find it in your heart to point out that they are almost right, as you explain the true facts.

The first President of the United States in Congress Assembled was Peyton Randolph, who took up office in 1774. The second President, John Hancock, signed the Declaration of Independence from Britain in 1776. There were twelve more Presidents before George Washington took up office in 1789, though he was the first President of the independent United States of America. So that's where your grown-up has got confused. Explain this slowly and carefully.

it's TRUE!

George Washington had troublesome teeth and by the time he became President he'd had almost all of them removed. He had false ones made from hippopotamus ivory as well as human teeth and the teeth of various other animals. There's a story that he wore wooden false teeth, but it isn't true.

Piranha fish will reduce a large mammal to a SKELETON in a matter of seconds

If you've ever been to an aquarium that keeps piranha fish, you might well have overheard adults saying this as though it were a biological fact rather than a complete load of old nonsense.

ACTUALLY, I'D MUCH RATHER HAVE A NICE BIT OF QUICHE.

There are many different types of piranha fish: some don't eat meat at all, and use their teeth for opening fruit and cracking nuts. Some piranha fish eat meat and have vicious-looking, interlocking teeth. The most fearsome of these is the red-bellied piranha, which is around 30 cm long and 3.5 kilos in weight. It lives on worms, fish and insects, and sometimes small mammals that have fallen into the water. It does not lie in wait in huge shoals for unsuspecting cows, jaguars or people to take a paddle. If you did wade into a shoal of red-bellied piranha in the Amazon River, you might get bitten if the fish were very hungry or if you had a cut somewhere on your body (piranha fish are good at sensing blood in the water). But usually piranhas would leave you alone – they don't see people as prey. On the other hand, just one bite from a hungry red-bellied piranha could amputate a finger, so it's not a great idea to swim in piranha-infested waters.

it's TRUE!

One type of piranha fish lives by nibbling the fins of other fish, which then swim away relatively unharmed.

some **PIRANHAS** are vegetarian

53

Human Body

If you shave, the hair will GROW back thicker

You would have thought the many bald grown-ups might be a sign that this is a load of nonsense.

Maybe some adults think this is true because a single hair is thinner at the end than it is at the base, which you can see if you compare a cut and an uncut hair very closely. Shaving doesn't cause hair to grow back thicker, more quickly, darker or anything else.

Shaving **DOESN'T** cause hair to **grow** **back** more quickly

HAIR MYTHS

* You can repair split ends (no, you can't!).

* Brushing your hair a hundred times before bed will make it shiny (it's not good for your hair to brush it that much).

* It's possible to turn grey overnight from shock (hair can turn grey quickly but it's not due to shock).

* Eating bread crusts makes your hair curly (see page 44).

* The more you wash your hair the more will fall out (for goodness' sake!).

INVENTIONS AND DISCOVERIES ⟨

Thomas CRAPPER invented the flush toilet

This is the kind of 'fact' that's bound to stick in the memory of a certain kind of grown-up (ones that didn't grow up very successfully), but of course it's not a fact at all.

Thomas Crapper lived in the 19th century, when he designed and made toilets and other bathroom ware. He did make some improvements to toilet design, but he certainly didn't invent flushing toilets. The first flushing toilets were used more than 4,000 years ago by the Indus Valley and Minoan civilizations. The Romans had flushing toilets too, but when their civilization came to an end, so did flushing loos. John Harrington, Queen Elizabeth I's godson, installed the first one in England for the Queen in 1597, but his invention wasn't much used until the 1700s, when the invention of the S-bend prevented nasty smells escaping from the sewers.

Even though he didn't invent them, Thomas Crapper's name did become well-known in the world of flushing toilets. But, in case you're wondering, he's not where the word 'crap' comes from – it comes from a very old English word meaning chaff (the husks of grain that are thrown away).

it's TRUE!

The first paper specifically designed and sold for use in the toilet went on sale in 1857.

The first
FLUSHING
toilets were
used more than
4,000
years ago

ANIMALS 🦆

One DOG year equals seven human years

Adults often say this. But you might ask them how come your year-old pet, Bonzo, is only seven when he looks nearly fully grown. The truth is that seven human years for every dog year doesn't really work.

The average lifespan of a dog is around 12 years. When they're a year old they're the equivalent of a teenager, and by two they're an adult in the prime of life. You could use a different formula to gauge your dog's age in human terms: the 15-10-5 rule makes your dog the equivalent of 15 human years after his first year of life, then, adding another ten, 25 human years at age two, then add five years for every dog year after that. So when your dog is four, he's 35 in human terms.

average lifespan of a dog is around 12 YEARS

AVERAGE ANIMAL AGES

GALAPAGOS LAND TORTOISE 193

AMAZON PARROT	80
HIPPOPOTAMUS	45
GORILLA	20
HOUSE MOUSE	4
MAYFLY	up to 1 day

FOOD AND DRINK 🥣

Certain foods make your BODY burn fat faster

Some grown-ups might tell you that particular foods help you burn fat faster — they might mention celery, or grapefruit, or maybe broccoli. Whichever food they mention as a 'fat-burner', they are talking complete rubbish.

No food can do this. A piece of CELERY or BROCCOLI doesn't contain many calories (and in fact you use up more calories eating and digesting celery than it contains), but that's not the same as making your body burn fat. **Exercise burns fat**, but eating grapefruit doesn't.

Calorie Counting

Average calories per 100g of...

Apple	47
Avocado	190
Bacon	257
Baked potato	136
Banana	95
Broccoli	24
Chicken breast	116
Celery	6
Chocolate	525
Crisps	500
Roast beef	136

HISTORY 📖

VIKINGS wore horned helmets

You sometimes see pictures of Vikings rampaging about waving axes and wearing scary looking helmets with horns sticking out of them. So perhaps we can't blame grown-ups for getting this one wrong ... on the other hand, maybe we can.

The Viking age started around the end of the 700s, when Viking raiders began attacking the coast of northern England. There's no evidence to suggest that the invaders were wearing horned helmets as they pillaged their way across Britain and Ireland – few Viking helmets have been found, and the ones that have are very ordinary pudding-basin style, without anything sticking out of them. A horned helmet has been unearthed by archaeologists in Denmark, and so have two Danish figurines of men wearing horned helmets, but they date from hundreds of years before the Vikings and archaeologists think the helmets were used for religious ceremonies. In the nineteenth century, painters looked back to Scandinavian myths for inspiration and decided to paint warriors wearing helmets with ox-like horns on them, perhaps because ancient Greek and Roman writers mentioned warriors wearing animal-horned headgear. Painters sometimes chose winged helmets instead. The paintings made the warriors look fierce and exotic, and helped continue the nonsense that many adults will tell you today.

vikings wore
PUDDING-BASIN
style helmets

VIKING FACTS

* The Vikings had some great nicknames: Ulf the Unwashed, Ragnar Hairy Breeches and Einer Belly-shaker, for example. A Viking slave might be known by a cruel nickname like Fat Legs, Stupid or Big Nose.

* Once every nine years at Uppsala in Sweden, the Vikings made an enormous sacrifice to their gods. Nine people were killed, together with nine of various different kinds of animal. The gruesome remains were hung from trees in a sacred grove.

* The word 'thing' comes from the Vikings. It meant a big meeting.

ULF THE UNWASHED

RAGNAR HAIRY BREECHES

ANIMALS

Bats are blind

Grown-ups might tell you that bats get about using echolocation and are completely blind. They might think they're clever because they know the word 'echolocation', but they are, of course, wrong about bats being blind.

Most bats don't have very good eyesight, but they can see. It's true that bats rely on echolocation to guide them rather than their vision: they make sounds of a very high frequency that reflect back to them, giving the creatures an accurate picture of the world around them. Fruit bats have better vision than most other bats and don't rely on echolocation so much.

By the way, if your adult tries to tell you that bats can get caught up in people's hair, they're wrong again. Bats can judge the location of a tiny insect with pinpoint accuracy so they're more than capable of flying around a person's head and hair.

it's TRUE!

* Bats are the only flying mammals in the world.

* There are more than 1,100 species of bat. They account for a quarter of all mammal species.

FRUIT BATS have BETTER VISION than most other bats

INVENTIONS AND DISCOVERIES

Nylon was named after NEW YORK and London

Even chemistry teachers sometimes get this one wrong.

Nylon was invented in 1935 by a chemist working for the American company Du Pont. He was trying to find a substitute for silk - the US imported it from Japan, but the two countries were becoming hostile towards one another. Before Du Pont put the new material on sale, it needed a name — polyhexamethyleneadipamide, its chemical name, seemed too much of a mouthful. They experimented with various words and came up with nylon, no one is quite sure why. Nylon first went on sale in 1939, launched in New York. London didn't have anything to do with its history.

> **it's TRUE!**
>
> Nylon was used to make toothbrushes, stockings, and all sorts of other things, but in its first five years it was used most to make parachutes - it was invented just before the outbreak of the Second World War. Now, nylon is mostly used to make carpets.

BONKERS! 🌀

If you have a black eye, putting a RAW STEAK on it will help it to get better

You have probably worked out for yourself that applying a piece of raw meat to an injury is more likely to make it much worse than to cure it.

A black eye is a bruise around the eye and is usually a minor injury (unless there are two black eyes, or other symptoms such as dizziness). Not much can be done about it, though gently applying an ice pack will help to reduce the swelling. Raw meat can contain harmful bacteria, especially if it isn't cold and people are handling it without washing their hands – the black eye could turn into a nasty infection.

RAW MEAT can contain harmful bacteria

CRAZY CURES

★ A Saxon cure for a stomach ache: Throw a beetle over your left shoulder

★ A medieval cure for a sore throat: Tie a string of worms around your neck

★ A Tudor cure for warts: Put half a mouse on the wart and bury the other half of the mouse

★ An 18th century cure for toothache: Apply squashed fish eyes

★ A 19th century cure for jaundice: Eat mice in red wine

ANIMALS 🐤

Dogs and cats are completely COLOUR blind

Ask your adult about the basis for this piece of scientific knowledge, then watch them try to weasel their way out of it.

Cats and dogs can see in colour, but not as many different colours as we can see. There are two types of light receptor in our eyes: rods and cones. Rods allow us to see when there isn't much light, but don't see colours. Three different types of cones allow us to see details and different colours (one type of cone deals with red colours, one green and one blue). Scientists think that cats and dogs have two different types of cone that show them the difference between red, blue and purple, but not other colours.

it's TRUE!

★ On average, about 9% of people are colour blind. The condition is much more common in men than in women.

★ Some animals can see colours people can't: spiders and insects can see ultraviolet light, and snakes can see infrared light.

HEALTH

It's DANGEROUS to wake a sleepwalker

Adults might tell you that sleepwalkers who are woken up are likely to die of shock on the spot. It's not true.

The sleepwalker is no more likely to have heart failure or some other kind of shock-related reaction than usual. But it can be quite difficult to wake up a sleepwalker and they might be disoriented or frightened and lash out at you. It's probably easier to guide them back to bed but if that fails and they're about to do something dangerous, like walk down a flight of stairs, it's better to just wake them up and risk being bashed.

> **It's TRUE!**
>
> People can do all sorts of things while sleepwalking: riding a bike, washing up, driving a car. In 2005, a 15-year-old girl climbed to the top of a 40-metre crane while she was asleep. She was discovered in the morning and had to be rescued by fire fighters.

Health

ST BERNARD dogs carry a bottle of brandy around their necks for victims of hypothermia

The St Bernard is a huge, bear-like breed of dog. The animals used to work as mountain-rescue dogs, sniffing out skiers in distress or avalanche victims. They're often pictured with a little barrel round their necks, and grown-ups will tell you that this contains brandy to help revive victims of hypothermia. Naturally, they are talking rubbish again.

Hypothermia sets in when the body becomes very cold and can no longer make up for the lost heat. Victims shiver violently and lose control of muscle movements – eventually they can die if they don't get help. Someone suffering from hypothermia needs to be warmed up gradually and given hot drinks (and anyone with severe hypothermia needs emergency medical attention). Victims should never be given alcohol of any kind – this will make their condition worse and in severe cases it could kill them. The reason St Bernard dogs were thought to carry brandy was because a nineteenth-century artist painted a picture of one of the dogs with a brandy barrel around its neck. There was no basis in reality for it; the artist just thought it looked good. But it lead to the myth that St Bernards carry brandy barrels.

sniffing out skiers in distress or avalanche VICTIMS

Big Dogs

	WEIGHT	HEIGHT (at shoulder)
Irish Wolfhound	47–57 kg	81–89 cm
Great Dane	45–54 kg	71–81 cm
English Mastiff	79–86 kg	69–76 cm
St Bernard	68–90 kg	69–76 cm

FOOD AND DRINK 🥣

It takes seven years to digest CHEWING gum

Adults don't want you to chew chewing gum, partly because they think they'll find it when you've finished with it and get a nasty surprise, and partly because they think you look like a slack-jawed idiot while you're chewing it (even though nothing could be further from the truth). So they come up with this sort of thing — even though it only makes them more likely to discover gum somewhere unexpected. They might also say if you swallow gum it gets entangled in your insides. They're fibbing again.

Chewing gum is made of gum resin (this can be either natural or synthetic), flavourings and sweeteners. The gum resin is indigestible, but that doesn't mean it lies in your stomach for seven years, or that it somehow gets caught up in your insides. It gets pushed through your system like any other piece of food, and comes out in the usual way.

On the other hand, it's not a good idea to swallow lots of gum. In rare cases, if you swallowed a lot of gum over a short period of time, it could block your stomach. But swallowing the odd bit of gum is harmless.

it's TRUE! Ancient Greeks, ancient Mayans, and various ancient North American tribes all chewed gum made from tree resin. The first commercial chewing gum went on sale in 1848, and bubble gum has been around since 1928. The record for the biggest bubble ever is 56 centimetres.

adults think you

look like a

SLACK-JAWED

idiot while you're

CHEWING

HUMAN BODY 🦶

The average person only uses 10% of his or her BRAIN

An adult might tell you this in an attempt to alert you to the wonderful untapped potential of your mighty brain, or maybe they're just repeating something they heard someone say without thinking about it too much. You might reply by suggesting that maybe **THEY** only use **10%** of **THEIR** brain, but you're pretty sure you use **100%** of yours.

Brain scans reveal that just about all the different parts of the brain are used by the average person during the course of a day. Of course, they might not all be in use at the same time – while you're sitting on the sofa watching telly, you might not be using the various bits of your brain that tell your hand to scratch your nose, or work out a maths problem, or climb a tree. Ask your adult what they mean when they say 10% of the brain – do they mean all of the brain is used, but only at 10% capacity (in which case, how would they or anyone else know?), or do they mean there's one area of the brain that's used while 90% of it isn't (which is plainly nonsense)?

There are plenty of fascinating facts about the brain, but this isn't one of them.

BRAINY FACTS

✴ The average human brain weighs 1.4 kg. It's already full size when you're eight years old.

✴ The surface of the brain, the cerebral cortex, stores information and allows us to think and remember. Each of its 15 billion brain cells make thousands of connections all the time, and the connections can change 200 times per second.

✴ There is a brain museum in Peru with a collection of nearly 3,000 brains. But the biggest brain collection in the world is at Harvard Brain Tissue Resource Center in the USA, which stores more than 6,500 brains.

SCIENCE

A penny dropped from a very tall BUILDING can kill a person on the ground below

Perhaps adults say this to stop you from throwing things off tall buildings, or perhaps they believe it's true. It isn't.

If there were no air, then the falling penny could well kill a person as it picked up more and more speed. But the penny meets resistance from the air, and tumbles as it falls because of its shape. A person on the ground would feel the penny hitting them, but it certainly wouldn't kill them.

Other things dropped from a tall building could well kill someone, though. The list of things you should never drop from a skyscraper is a long one, and includes potted begonias (because they're heavy), pens (because they are aerodynamically shaped), and sheep (for obvious reasons).

Tall Buildings

The world's tallest structure is the Burj Dubai in Dubai, United Arab Emirates, which measures 818 metres. Other very tall things include...

WHAT	WHERE	HEIGHT
Petronas Towers	Kuala Lumpur, Malaysia	452 metres
Sears Tower	Chicago, USA	442 metres
Jin Mao Building	Shanghai, China	421 metres
Empire State Building	New York, USA	381 metres

80

STATISTICS

You're more likely to be killed by a COCONUT hitting you on the head than by a shark attack

This is the kind of thing adults find on the Internet then repeat to anyone who will listen, assuming that if they read it on the Internet, it must be true. It isn't.

An average of about five people are killed every year by sharks. This is very few. But it's at least 20 times more than the victims of falling coconuts. People have been killed when coconuts fell from palm trees and hit them on the head, but they are very rare cases. There have been one or two reports of coconut-related deaths, but statistics are hard to find.

The story about deadly coconuts seems to have begun with a statement from a holiday insurance company, when a spokesman claimed that 150 people were killed each year by falling coconuts. Could the company have wanted fearful customers to take out insurance policies for their trips to coconut-growing countries? Then again, wouldn't it have been easier to make people more afraid of sharks?

On the other hand,
it's always a good
idea to be cautious –
NEVER have
a nap in the shade of
a COCONUT PALM

it's TRUE!

From 1990 to 2008 there were 57 shark attacks per year, on average, worldwide. An average of five of them were fatal. The world's number-one shark attack location is Florida in the United States, where a third of the attacks from 1990 to 2008 happened.

BONKERS! 🌀

If you cross your eyes they can become STUCK that way

Either some grown-ups have a massive sense of humour problem and just can't see that pulling funny faces is absolutely hilarious, or they are being deliberately vindictive to small children. They might also use a variation on this grown-up fib: 'If you pull a face and the wind changes, you'll stay that way.' Tell them they should get out more and gurn as much as you like.

It's TRUE!

If you like pulling faces, why not take part in the World Gurning Championship? It takes place every September in Cumbria, as part of the Egremont Crab Fair.

HISTORY 📖

Admiral Horatio NELSON had only one eye

Many adults are convinced that Nelson had one arm and one eye and wore an eye patch. But they're (mostly) wrong.

Nelson damaged his right eye during a naval battle. He couldn't see out of it very well, but it was still there, it wasn't blind, and he didn't cover it up with an eye patch. After his death, paintings of Nelson sometimes show him wearing an eye patch, perhaps in an effort to show how heroic he was. The statue at the top of Nelson's column doesn't show him wearing an eye patch, though it does show an empty sleeve – his right arm was amputated after it had been shattered in the Battle of Santa Cruz, Tenerife.

> **it's TRUE!**
>
> Nelson died at the Battle of Trafalgar in 1805 and his body was put in a barrel of brandy to stop it from rotting on the journey back to England. The story goes that sailors stuck straws into the barrel and drank the brandy.

SCIENCE

In summertime the Earth is closer to the SUN than in winter

It's easy to see why some grown-ups get confused about this. Take pity on them and explain carefully.

The sun is no nearer to the Earth in summer. The Earth is tilted on its axis. For six months of the year the northern hemisphere is tilted towards the sun (see diagram on p.86) – this is some of springtime, all of summertime, and a bit of autumn in the northern hemisphere. The other six months of the year the southern hemisphere is tilted towards the sun – and in the middle of that is the southern hemisphere's summer.

The SUN is no nearer to the EARTH in summer

The Earth orbits the sun not in a perfect circle but an oval, with the sun off centre slightly. So at one time of year the Earth actually does pass more closely to the sun – in January. It's furthest away from the sun in July – even though that's summer in the northern hemisphere.

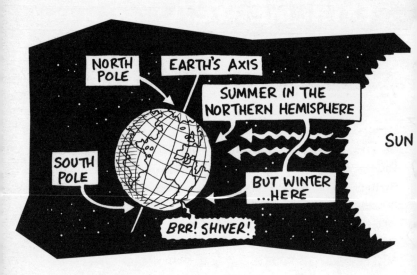

EXTREME WEATHER

✴ The highest temperature recorded on Earth was 70.7 °C in the Lut desert, Iran.

✴ The heaviest hailstones fell on Bangladesh in 1986 - each weighed over 1 kg. The largest hailstone ever recorded fell on Nebraska, USA, and measured nearly 17.8 cm in diameter.

✴ The heaviest snowfall in one year was measured at 31.1 metres. It fell on Mount Rainier, USA in 1972.

PLACES 🌐

HAGGIS and porridge come from Scotland

Even Scottish adults can get this wrong.

A haggis is a sheep's insides mixed with oatmeal, onion and suet encased in the sheep's stomach. It might not sound very appetizing but people have been eating it for a long time in many different parts of the world. The earliest haggis was around in Ancient Greece. So the Scots definitely weren't the first.

At one time most human beings ate porridge made from oats. It's been found in the stomachs of preserved bodies from thousands of years ago, in Europe and Scandinavia. It was probably invented in China.

> **it's TRUE!**
>
> Not even bagpipes are Scottish by origin: they were probably invented in central Asia thousands of years ago. The instrument was introduced to Britain by the Romans.

FOOD AND DRINK 🍲

Eating CHOCOLATE gives you spots

Some grown-ups will stop at nothing to deprive you of life's little pleasures. No, chocolate doesn't give you spots. Neither does pizza, dairy products or crisps, or any other specific food. And if an adult tells you that greasy foods cause greasy skin, don't listen to them: that's not true either.

There are various different reasons for getting spots, such as a hormone imbalance (common in teenagers), or overactive oil-producing glands. Some research suggests a healthy diet, with lots of fruit and vegetables, leads to healthier skin – but there's no particular food that can be blamed for spots.

it's TRUE!

The Mayan people of South America made a bitter, spicy drink out of cocoa beans. Spanish conquerors brought it to Spain, where it was mixed with sugar and vanilla. Over time it became popular to eat chocolate as well as drink it.

No, chocolate doesn't give you SPOTS

ANIMALS 🐤

If you cut a WORM in half, both halves will live

Kind-hearted adults might tell you this to make you feel better about chopping up worms with your trowel: they're lying again, whether they realize it or not.

If you cut an earthworm in half, you don't get two worms. Usually, you get one dead one in two pieces. The half with the head might live, as long as it has enough of its body to go with it (half of its body isn't enough). The tail end definitely won't live. Gruesomely, each half might writhe about after it's been chopped for quite some time, but this doesn't mean the worm's hale and hearty or doing a little dance or something – it means it's dying.

it's TRUE!

The world's largest earthworms live in Australia – the giant Gippsland earthworms can be four metres long.

91

INVENTIONS AND DISCOVERIES

John Logie Baird INVENTED television

If you want to be kind to your adult, you could tell them that this is a common mistake that many grown-ups make.

Scottish inventor John Logie Baird has become famous for inventing television but he didn't invent an electronic one (which is how today's tellies work) and he might not have been the first to make a television of any sort, either. John Logie Baird gave a public demonstration of his mechanical television in London in 1926 – around the same time, various people in other countries were doing similar things. Baird was good at publicity, though, and became known as the Television Man, which is probably why so many people credit him with the invention.

Baird didn't INVENT an electronic television

Really there's no single inventor of television — many people made improvements and advances in the first part of the twentieth century. The American Philo Taylor Farnsworth, and Russian Vladimir Zworkin both developed electronic televisions that formed the basis of modern ones.

it's TRUE!

John Logie Baird invented other things as well as televisions: he tried to create diamonds using carbon and electricity, he invented and sold the Baird Undersock (basically a foot-powdered sock), and he also experimented with making a rustless razor, which cut him, and pneumatic shoes, which burst.

BONKERS! ◎

Eating an APPLE cleans your teeth

If an adult tells you this, the chances are they're quite old ... and have false teeth. Most adults – even the simpler ones – know that cleaning your teeth does not involve eating anything, it involves a toothbrush. But in days gone by, people didn't know as much about dental hygiene as they do now. Believe it or not, many people grew up believing that eating an apple would freshen their breath and clean their teeth. If your granny or great-granny tells you this, it's probably too late to enlighten them.

> **it's TRUE!**
>
> Sugar isn't good for your teeth, and that includes the sugar contained in apples and other fruit, as well as sweets. But things don't have to be sweet to be bad for your teeth: crisps, crackers and cereal are much better at clinging to your teeth than sugar and can be just as bad, or even worse, if you don't brush regularly.

VITAMIN C will stop you from catching a COLD

How often have you heard grown-ups come out with this one? Yet again, they are talking rubbish.

Colds are caused by viruses, which can be transmitted from person to person in a number of ways. Vitamin C is no protection against them. In 2007, researchers at the Australian National University and the University of Helsinki studied a group of more than 11,000 people. They concluded that a daily dose of Vitamin C didn't stop people getting colds, though it could slightly reduce how long they lasted. There is some evidence to suggest that people exposed to periods of very high physical stress, like marathon runners, can reduce their chances of catching a cold by taking Vitamin C. But most of us don't run marathons.

In the 1970s a Nobel-Prize winning scientist called Linus Pauling suggested that people should take a huge 1,000 mg Vitamin C supplement every day to ward off colds. He is probably responsible for people thinking that Vitamin C stops you catching a cold, but he is just another adult who was plain wrong.

It's TRUE!

A lack of Vitamins C and B leads to the disease scurvy. Since sailors didn't have much access to Vitamin-packed fresh fruit and vegetables on board ship before the 19th century, many of them died of scurvy. Eventually a doctor made the link between fresh produce and scurvy, and sailors were supplied with lemon juice.

Vitamin C IS NO PROTECTION AGAINST COLDS

HUMAN BODY 🦴

It takes more MUSCLES to smile than it does to frown

This is a bit like saying, 'Now, turn that frown upside down!' which can be a little irritating, especially if you've just discovered you've failed all your exams, lost £10 or been dumped. The grown-up who says this is really trying to say that it's easier to be happy than to be sad, but, at least in terms of frowns, smiles and facial muscles, they are once again wrong.

a genuine SMILE INVOLVES 12 different muscles

A miserable frown involves 11. An insincere raising of the corners of the mouth only uses two muscles, but we can safely assume this isn't the sort of smile in question. Whether it takes less effort to frown than to smile is down to the individual – whether they frown more often or smile more often, and whether they're generally a misery guts.

SUNNY DISPOSITION   MISERABLE GIT

Dying of Laughter

Laughing is good for you, and laughter therapy can be used to relieve stress. But beware – people have been known to die laughing:

* A man died laughing at a comedy TV programme called 'The Goodies' in 1975. The scene involved a Scotsman in a kilt fending off an attacking black pudding with his bagpipes.

* A comedy musical play called 'The Beggar's Opera' claimed a victim in 1782. A woman started laughing when a comic actor first appeared, and she had to leave the theatre when she couldn't stop. In fact she didn't stop laughing until she died the following morning.

* The King of Burma, Nanda Bayin, died laughing in 1599 when he was told that Venice was a free state with no monarch. Apparently, he found the idea hilarious.

BONKERS! ⊚

If you pick your NOSE your brain will cave in

Honestly! Some adults clearly think children are just idiots. Either that or they're talking to two-year-olds – in which case, isn't it just cruel?

Picking your nose is pretty disgusting, it's true, but it won't do you any real harm as long as you don't do it too often or too vigorously and wash your hands afterwards.

And you can rest assured that it won't make your brain cave in.

it's TRUE!

Compulsive nose picking is known as rhinotillexomania.

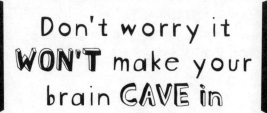

Don't worry it **WON'T** make your brain **CAVE** in

100

HISTORY 📖

Saint George was ENGLISH

Your adult could be forgiven for this one: Saint George is England's patron saint. But, of course, he wasn't English.

Not much is known about Saint George at all, but you can be pretty sure he wasn't born in England. He lived during the third century and was born (probably) in Cappadocia, which is now part of Turkey. Your adult might also be interested to know that Saint George is also the patron saint of Lithuania, Portugal, Germany and Greece, amongst other places.

Saint George wasn't born in ENGLAND

UNUSUAL PATRON SAINTS

* Saint Drogo, patron saint of ugly people

* Saint Ambrose, patron saint of bee keepers

* Saint Anthony the Abbot, patron saint of eczema

* Saint Marin of Tours, patron saint of geese

* Saint Gabriel the Archangel, patron saint of stamp collectors

PLACES 🌐

BOOMERANGS originated in Australia

Boomerangs are hunting sticks — some of them return to the hunter after they've been thrown, if they're thrown correctly, while others are for throwing and retrieving later. Most adults know they come from Australia originally. But they're wrong.

Australian Aborigines are famous for boomerangs, but they weren't the first people in the world to develop them. The oldest boomerangs that have ever been found are 18,000 years old – a returning hunting stick was found in a cave in the Carpathian Mountains of Poland. The oldest Australian boomerang ever found is around 10,000 years old.

The word boomerang does come from Australia, though. The Turuwal Aboriginal people, from modern-day New South Wales, used the word to describe hunting sticks that return to the hunter (as opposed to throwing sticks that don't come back).

it's TRUE!

The didgeridoo, one of the oldest wind instruments in the world, DOES come from Australia. It's been played by Aboriginal people for at least 1,500 years. A 2005 medical study suggested that playing the didgeridoo regularly helps reduce snoring, because of the special breathing techniques needed to play it.

Boomerangs are hunting sticks that RETURN to the hunter

Health 👁

You should suck VENOM out of a snake bite and spit it out

If you watch enough old cowboy films you're bound to see someone being bitten on the ankle by a rattlesnake and having the venom sucked out by a trusted friend. Maybe this is the reason so many adults think this is a useful piece of medical advice.

Snakes are venomous, not poisonous – they inject venom into other creatures' bodies with their fangs. Poisonous animals are harmful if eaten. Sucking out venom from a snake bite isn't necessarily going to hurt the person doing the sucking – unless they have a wound inside their mouth, in which case the venom could enter their bloodstream and they would be in as much trouble as the person bitten by the snake. Every human mouth is laden with germs, however, and that is not likely to be good for a bite wound. Also, in order to get the poison out, the snake bite needs to be opened with something sharp, and this is definitely not a good idea. Even if someone with sterilized surgical equipment, who had just visited the dentist, opened a snake bite and sucked out the poison, it still wouldn't be the best thing to do. Venom from a snake bite can travel around the body extremely quickly and anything that increases the heart rate – like someone wielding a rusty knife – is going to make it travel faster. The best thing to do is to keep the victim calm, keep the bite wound below the heart, and call for emergency help.

they **INJECT** VENOM into other creatures' bodies with their **fangs**.

it's TRUE!

The Inland Taipan, found in Australia, has the most toxic venom of any snake in the world. It's not the most deadly snake, though. The Carpet Viper, found in Africa and Asia, probably kills the most people.

ANIMALS 🐥

A CENTIPEDE has 100 legs

Your adult has been confused by the 'cent' part of the word centipede, which means 100 in Latin, but in this case just means 'lots'.

Centipedes have anything between 15 and 191 pairs of legs. Most have an odd number of pairs, there's only one type that has an even number – 48 – giving 96 legs, which is the closest any centipede comes to having 100.

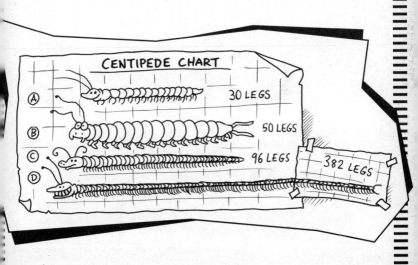

CENTIPEDE CHART

ⓐ 30 LEGS
ⓑ 50 LEGS
ⓒ 96 LEGS
ⓓ 382 LEGS

it's TRUE!

The world's largest centipede is the Amazonian giant centipede, which can be more than 30 cm long. It eats small animals, such as lizards, spiders, insects and mice, and it dangles from the roofs of caves to catch bats in mid-flight. It has between 42 and 46 legs.

CENTIPEDES have anything between 15 and 191 PAIRS OF LEGS

SCIENCE

Air is mostly OXYGEN

Many grown-ups seem to have had a woefully inadequate scientific education, and this is a glaring example.

Air is not mostly oxygen; it's mostly nitrogen, which makes up a whopping great 78% of the air. Oxygen accounts for 21%. The other 1% is made up of very small amounts of argon, neon helium, krypton, xenon, hydrogen, carbon dioxide, methane, nitrous oxide, water vapour and ozone. If you can remember all of those you will seriously impress any adult.

it's TRUE!

Some of the gases present in the atmosphere give out coloured light when they are electrically charged. Neon is used to fill tubes for colourful neon signs and can also be used in lasers. Lasers also use krypton. Xenon is used in incandescent lighting, x-rays and other medical imaging.

ANIMALS

A column of ARMY ANTS will reduce you to a skeleton within minutes if you are in its path

This looks like another 'fact' adults have gleaned from watching a lot of old films. It seems they must have spent far too much time in front of the telly when they were children.

A swarm of army ants can number millions. Even so, you've no need to be frightened of it. Unless you are completely unable to move, and there's no help at hand, you can avert disaster by simply walking away. They travel at about 20 metres an hour – even if you're very unfit you should be able to do better than that. There are various different kinds of army ant, which live in Africa and Central and South America and feed on insects and small animals.

it's TRUE!

Soldier ants in a column of army ants can give a nasty bite. But bullet ants have an extremely painful bite - it's compared to the pain of being shot with a bullet, and lasts up to 24 hours.

A SWARM
of army ants
can number
millions

SPACE

Meteors are falling STARS

Really, grown-ups: it's not that difficult...

A meteor appears as a streak of light flashing briefly through the night sky. Sometimes they're called 'shooting stars'. But they have nothing to do with stars. A meteor is seen when a lump of metal or rock (known as a meteoroid) enters the Earth's atmosphere. Friction from the air heats it up, causing it to glow as it burns up in the atmosphere. If a meteoroid falls to Earth without being burned up in the atmosphere, it's called a meteorite.

it's TRUE!

Most meteors are caused by a meteoroid the size of a pebble. Meteor showers happen at particular times every year, when the Earth meets groups of meteoroids: for example, the Leonid shower can be seen every November, and the Perseid shower happens in August.

ANIMALS 🐱

Violin strings are made from CAT GUT

Little do adults know that they are continuing a myth started centuries ago by Italian violin makers. Rest assured, you don't need to worry about Tiddles.

Violin strings have never been made from cat gut, not even in the dim and distant past when all sorts of animal bits and pieces were used for all sorts of things. Italian violin makers began producing some of the best violin strings during the Middle Ages – they used sheep gut. But they told everyone they used cat gut because they didn't want anyone else to copy them – killing cats was considered to be extremely bad luck. Violin strings continued to be made from sheep gut until the middle of the 18th century. Today, gut strings are still available, along with nylon and steel strings.

it's TRUE!

People have been playing music for a very long time. The oldest musical instrument ever found was a 9,000-year-old flute, made from a bone, discovered in China.

Violin STRINGS have never been made from cat gut

FOOD AND DRINK 🥣

Brown eggs are more NUTRITIOUS than white ones

Adults like to think they are positively influencing your health and well being. But they aren't if they tell you this.

First of all, just to be clear, we're talking about chicken eggs, rather than ostrich eggs or crocodile eggs. Brown eggs are laid by brown or reddish coloured chickens. White eggs are laid by white chickens. There's no difference in the quality of the eggs. One kind is not better for you than the other. So it doesn't matter – one less thing to bother about.

> **It's TRUE!**
>
> The largest known egg in the world belongs to the now extinct Great Elephant Bird. The egg measures 33 centimetres tall and a metre in circumference, 300 times the size of a chicken's egg, and is the biggest egg laid by any creature, including dinosaurs. The Great Elephant Bird was huge - more than 3 metres tall and half a tonne in weight. It lived in Madagascar and was wiped out in the 1600s.

INVENTIONS AND DISCOVERIES ◁

James Watt INVENTED the steam engine

Grown-ups are wrong about this one by about 1,700 years.

The steam engine was invented in ancient Greece around AD 50. But the ancient Greeks didn't use it to power boats or machines – they had lots of slaves to do things for them, and Hero, the inventor of the steam engine, used it to power little toys instead. Then it was forgotten about for ages. In 1698 Thomas Savery invented a steam pump, and in 1712 Thomas Newcomen built a steam engine. In the late 1700s, James Watt improved on Newcomen's engine so much that it really did change things, and meant that steam engines were much more efficient and could be used safely and in lots of different ways. So even though Watt didn't actually invent the steam engine, he deserves plenty of credit.

> **it's TRUE!**
>
> As well as giving his name to a unit of power that you see on light bulbs, James Watt came up with the term 'horsepower'.

Bonkers! ⊚

You swallow eight SPIDERS every year in your sleep

It's amazing but true: adults will believe anything they read on the internet.

In 1993, a journalist wrote about the various different lists of 'facts' that were circulating on the Internet, and how they got passed on via email until lots of people believed a lot of made-up nonsense. To make her point, she created her own list, and one of her made-up 'facts' was that we all swallow eight spiders a year in our sleep. She got it from an old book of popular misconceptions about insects. Of course, then her own list was copied and circulated on the Internet ... until lots of people believed yet another piece of made-up nonsense.

Of course, you might swallow spiders in your sleep. But how would you know, unless you woke up with a long, dangly leg sticking out of your mouth, or unless you videoed yourself every single night as you slept. But they'd have to be very small spiders, without much of a survival instinct.

it's TRUE!

People deliberately eat insects and spiders in many different parts of the world. In Asia, tarantula spiders are served fried and dipped in garlic and salt.

you **might** SWALLOW spiders in your SLEEP

HISTORY 📖

Medieval explorers thought the world was FLAT

Plenty of adults think this is true, and some will tell you that Columbus made his voyage across the Atlantic in **1492** to prove that the Earth wasn't flat. But people at the time didn't believe they would fall off the end of the Earth if they sailed too far.

People had believed the Earth was a sphere from ancient times. More than 2,200 years ago, an ancient Greek called Eratosthenes even worked out its circumference (and was pretty accurate). In the Middle Ages the Church was adamant that the Earth was in the centre of the Universe with the Sun orbiting around it, and got very annoyed with Copernicus's Sun-centred Universe, but no one was saying that the Earth was flat. When Columbus set off on his journey westwards from Spain, he didn't think there was any chance of sailing off the edge of the world and plummeting into space, and neither did any of his crew. There were plenty of maps and Columbus knew all about Eratosthenes' calculations.

it's TRUE!

Christopher Columbus wanted to make the shape of the Earth fit in with his idea that he could reach India from Spain by sailing west. So he made it much smaller than Eratosthenes had accurately calculated, and theorized that it must be slightly pear-shaped.

Today there is an organization called the **Flat Earth Society**, set up under a different name in the 19th century, whose few hundred members **believe** that the EARTH ISN'T A SPHERE.

HEALTH 👁

Touching a TOAD can give you warts

Some grown-ups might as well be living in the Middle Ages. If you know one who believes that toads give you warts, sigh heavily and explain the true facts.

Warts are bumpy growths on the skin, most commonly found on people's hands. They're a common skin infection caused by a virus, and they are contagious – they can be passed on by touch from person to person (but not from toad to person, or person to toad). Treatments for getting rid of warts involve freezing them or burning them. If warts are left alone they usually go away on their own, though this can take a long time.

It could be that toads got the blame for causing warts because toads have bumpy skin. Some toads have poisonous glands on the skin that can cause a reaction on human skin that could be confused with a wart. Whatever the reason for the confusion, toads definitely cannot give you warts. Let's stop blaming them now! And, by the way, warts do not have 'roots' – that's another lie.

it's TRUE!

Occasionally it rains frogs and toads – it happened in Birmingham, England, in 1954, in the town of Villa Angel Flores, Mexico, in 1997, and in June 2009 rains of tadpoles occurred in the Ishikawa district of Japan.

If WARTS are left alone they usually GO AWAY

ANIMALS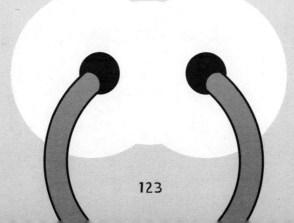

Bulls are INCENSED by the colour red

Many adults are quite convinced of this. They even have an expression about it: 'like a red rag to a bull', which might lead you to think that bulls can only see red, or that they attack the colour red.

In fact bulls can distinguish between a few different colours. They can see the colour red but, like cats and dogs, they might confuse red with green or yellow. The idea that bulls can only see red probably arose because of a matador's red cape in a bull fight. It's not the colour red that bothers them – it's the movement of the cloth ... and the knives embedded in its back.

HOW TO ESCAPE FROM AN ANGRY BULL

✳ Don't panic, and don't run away – the bull might well chase you.

✳ Stay still. Bulls don't have very good eyesight, though their hearing and sense of smell are excellent. If you keep still the bull will probably lose interest.

✳ If the bull charges at you, you have no choice but to run. Unfortunately the bull can run faster than you. Look out for a tree to climb or a building or fence to hide in or behind.

✳ As you run, take off items of clothing and throw them to the side – hopefully, the bull will investigate.

SCIENCE ✶

WATER goes down the plug hole one way in the northern hemisphere and the opposite direction in the southern hemisphere

If an adult tells you this, ask them why and watch them squirm.

Just to clear things up at the beginning, it isn't true. The water will swirl down the plughole either clockwise or anticlockwise depending on the position of the plughole, the angle of the sink, and other factors. But it has nothing to do with which hemisphere it's in. Whether you're in Paris or Sydney, the water could swirl down the plughole either way.

It's the Coriolis force, an effect of the Earth's rotation, that seems to have caused confusion about plugholes. A large object, such as a mass of air, moving above the Earth towards the north or south is deflected by the Coriolis force - clockwise in the northern hemisphere and anticlockwise in the southern hemisphere. But the force only acts on large objects travelling long distances – it doesn't affect ships at sea, or the water in your plughole.

HISTORY

Captain Cook DISCOVERED Australia

Grown-ups aren't even close on this one. Patiently tell them what really happened.

50,000 years ago, the Aboriginal people became the first to live in Australia. At this point your adult will probably protest that they meant 'apart from them'. It's not certain who reached Australia next – possibly Indonesian traders or Chinese explorers.

The first European to reach Australia was Dutchman William Janszoon, who landed there in 1606.

After Janszoon, explorers from various different European countries visited Australia, including Englishman William Dampier, who got there more than 70 years before Cook.

Lieutenant James Cook (he wasn't a captain yet) arrived in Australia in 1770, charted the east coast, and claimed it for England. He was the first European to make maps of the eastern coast of Australia, but that's not quite the same as discovering the entire continent, as your adult will have to agree.

it's TRUE!

Captain Cook died in 1771 on the island of Hawaii, killed by Hawaiian islanders after Cook had kidnapped their king. Various bits of Cook were sent by the islanders to Cook's ship - they received various gruesome packages containing a thigh, feetless legs, the hands and the arms (separately), the skull and the scalp.

He was the **first** European to make MAPS of the eastern coast of Australia

FOOD AND DRINK

Eating CARROTS helps you see in the dark

This isn't exactly true, but you could be kind and tell your misguided adult that they're almost right.

It's true that Vitamin A is essential for healthy eyesight, and it's also true that carrots contain plenty of Vitamin A. If you had a deficiency of Vitamin A, your night vision would be poor, so eating Vitamin-A rich carrots might help you. Apricots and spinach contain even more Vitamin A than carrots, so eating those would be even better. Most people don't have a deficiency of Vitamin A, though, so eating carrots (or apricots or spinach) wouldn't make any difference at all. It's certainly not true that the more carrots you eat, the better your night vision.

The connection between carrots and seeing in the dark came about because of a propaganda story during World War Two. The British Ministry of Food let it be known that eating carrots helped night vision to explain why their pilots seemed

128

to have become better at spotting German planes. The real reason was that they had developed radar, but they didn't want their enemies to know that. The story had the added benefit of getting everyone to eat more easy-to-grow vegetables.

it's TRUE!

Carrots used to be popular in many different colours - white, red, yellow and purple ones. Orange carrots were first bred in Holland to honour the Dutch royal family, the House of Orange. Orange carrots contain beta-carotine, which can turn your skin orange if you eat a lot of carrots over a long period of time.

TRY IT YOURSELF

... and find out it doesn't work

✳ Test your night vision using a sight chart in a darkened room

✳ Eat 5 carrots a day for a week

✳ Test your night vision again

✳ Discover that there is no difference

✳ Be alarmed by your orange skin, especially on your palms and the soles of your feet

HISTORY 📖

The nursery rhyme 'Ring-a-Ring o' Roses' is about the PLAGUE

It's amazing how many adults will tell you this, thinking they're in possession of an interesting historical fact. They might elaborate by saying that the 'rings' were the spots that were a telltale sign a person had the plague, that people wore 'posies' to ward off the disease ('A pocketful of posies' is the second line of the rhyme), before sneezing violently ('Atishoo, atishoo,') and then dying ('We all fall down'). They're wrong.

The Great Plague struck Europe in the 1600s, arriving in England in the 1660s. Some people claim the rhyme is about the Black Death, which killed millions in Europe in the 1300s. The first recorded version of 'Ring-a-ring o' Roses' dates from America in 1790 (though of course this doesn't tell us where and when it began to be used). There are many different versions of the rhyme, in different countries from America to Germany. Some of them have second verses where everyone jumps up again, some of them don't mention falling down at all, and several refer to ringing bells, steeples,

Jack, Jim, Moses or Josie. The rhyme could have been around since the time of the Great Plague, but there's nothing to suggest that it's about the disease. The first time anyone suggested the rhyme was about the plague was in the 20th century. So it looks as though your adult has been talking nonsense again.

There were various 'cures' for the GREAT PLAGUE...

* Smoke tobacco.

* Apply the blood of a pigeon to plague sores.

* Wear a dead toad around your neck.

* Apply the tail feathers of a live chicken to plague sores to draw out the poison.

PEOPLE 🧠

ESKIMOS rub noses instead of kissing

Your confused grown-up has probably got this from a cartoon or an old film.

By the way, Eskimos are people who live in the Arctic regions of Alaska, Canada and Greenland. The people of northern Canada and parts of Greenland prefer to be called Inuit, although Alaskan Eskimos and some from Greenland are not Inuit, but one of a number of other nationalities (including the Aleut, Yakut, Yupiit and Sami people), and so they would rather be called Eskimo than Inuit (and, presumably, even more pleased if you bothered to find out their actual nationality).

Eskimos are people who live in the Arctic regions of Alaska, Canada and Greenland

Eskimos do have a form of greeting or affection called kunik, often used between adults and children, where they put their nose and top lip against someone's skin and sniff. But it's nothing to do with rubbing noses, and they don't do it instead of kissing.

it's TRUE!

The area around the North Pole, the Arctic Circle, includes parts of Canada, Greenland, Russia, Alaska, Iceland, Norway, Sweden and Finland. Although you can walk to the North Pole (if you're wearing plenty of warm clothes), you're not walking on land but on a thick layer of ice.

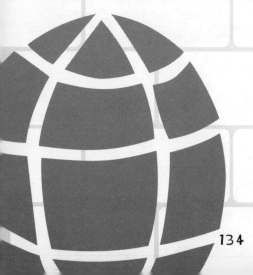

HEALTH

If you go outside with wet hair you'll catch a COLD

Most people, even adults who say things like this, realize that colds are caused by viruses, not by the temperature. Perhaps they think that having wet hair makes you cold, which makes you more likely to catch a cold. But they're wrong.

Making your body cold can make you more likely to become ill, but only if you're really cold. You'd probably need to go out with wet hair and no clothes on in the middle of winter for this to happen. Various studies have been carried out and they all lead to the conclusion that being a bit cold, or having wet hair on a cold day, will not make you any more likely to catch a cold.

The reason people tend to get more colds in the winter months isn't because of the temperature — it's because we tend to stay indoors more, in closer contact with other people and their coughs and sneezes...

COLDS are caused by VIRUSES, not by the temperature

It's TRUE!

* When you sneeze, particles fly out of your nose at astonishing speeds - up to 100 mph.

* The germs from your sneeze can travel up to a metre.

INVENTIONS AND DISCOVERIES

George Stephenson invented the steam LOCOMOTIVE

It's shocking how many grown-ups were misinformed during their school days.

By the time George Stephenson turned his attention to steam locomotives, several of them already existed. They weren't very good, though – they were heavy, slow, inefficient and kept breaking down or falling off their rails. George designed his own steam engines, and made huge improvements. His first steam engine was called Blucher (it wasn't Rocket, as some grown-ups might tell you). He won a competition to find a workable steam locomotive with his locomotive Rocket, which beat the other engines easily and began the story of railways. Stephenson even designed the first railway system.

it's TRUE! Rocket could pull a carriage full of passengers at 39 km/h. The fastest ever steam locomotive was the Mallard, built in 1938. Its top speed was an impressive 202 km/h.

HISTORY 📖

Marie Antoinette said, 'Let them eat CAKE!'

This is yet another historical 'fact' that adults hope to impress you with — until you tell them they're completely wrong.

Marie Antoinette was the Queen of France at the time of the French Revolution, during which she was guillotined. She's supposed to have said the words, 'Let them eat cake' when she was told that the poor people of France didn't have enough bread to eat, showing her complete ignorance of how people lived - she had no idea that they couldn't just go and get some cake instead when they ran out of baguette. In other words, she was a decadent royal idiot who deserved to have her head chopped off.

However, the phrase 'let them eat cake' had already been used, attributed to various other French aristocrats, long before the French Revolution. It might have been made up, to highlight the vast difference between rich and poor, and not actually said by anyone. By the time Marie Antoinette was trying to run away from the revolting peasants, 'Let them eat cake' had been used as an illustration of idiot aristocrats for some time, so she wouldn't have said it.

It's TRUE!

During the Reign of Terror in the French Revolution, from 1793-94, many thousands of people were guillotined - at least 16,000 but possibly as many as 40,000.

'LET them eat cake'

GEOGRAPHY

The last ICE AGE happened thousands of years ago

Grown-ups are often confused about this one, and it's not difficult to see why. You could point that out during your patient explanation.

The Earth has gone through various warm and cold periods in its long history. An ice age is, of course, one of the cold periods, when both of the Earth's poles are covered in ice. It can last for millions of years. In fact, if you check on the current condition of the North and South Poles, you'll see that we're in the middle of an ice age right now. We're having a warmer phase in our current ice age – between 10,000 and 30,000 years ago, there was a colder phase, and the glaciers reached down into Europe and North America. This is what a lot of grown-ups refer to as the ice age. Really it was just a colder period in the current one.

It's TRUE!

If all the land ice on Earth melted, the sea level would rise by about 70 metres.

HUMAN BODY

Hair and nails continue to GROW after death

Many adults will tell you this particular untruth without ever having seen a dead body. It sounds creepy, but it's not true.

After death, all sorts of gruesome things do happen to the human body. One of them is dehydration. The lack of water in the body causes it to shrink, and this can make it seem as if nails and hair have got longer. It's not true: the body has shrunk, rather than the hair and nails lengthening.

IT'S TRUE!

Egyptian mummies have suffered all sorts of indignities over the centuries. In the 19th century bits of them were used as medicine, or mixed into dye in a paint colour called 'mummy brown'. Mummies were also dissected as audiences watched, in events known as 'unrollings'. In 1907, when land was cleared for the Aswan Dam in Egypt, thousands of mummies were burnt.

HISTORY 📖

Lady Godiva rode NAKED through the streets of Coventry

A lot of adults confuse historical fact with legend, and this is the case with Lady Godiva.

The story goes that Lady Godiva, a noblewoman married to Leofric, pleaded with her husband to stop demanding the unfair taxes he was taking from the people of Coventry. Eventually he said he would do so if she rode naked through the town. So she did, telling everyone not to peek, keeping their windows shuttered and their doors closed. One man, Peeping Tom, made a hole in his window shutter and had a peek, and as a result he was struck blind.

There really was a Lady Godiva, married to Leofric, Earl of Mercia. She lived in the 1000s and gets a mention in William the Conqueror's Domesday Book. But there's no evidence to suggest she rode naked through the streets of Coventry, or that she got her husband to reduce everyone's taxes (or that anyone was struck blind for looking at a naked woman on a horse).

it's TRUE!

The Domesday Book is a record of all property-owning people, their land, property and animals, and how much they were worth, in England. It was made in 1085-1086 on the orders of King William I (William the Conqueror), so that he could tax people more effectively. It contains more than two million words (in Latin) and describes 13,000 places in England and parts of Wales.

NO evidence
to suggest she
rode naked through
the streets of
Coventry

SPACE

The North Star, or Pole Star, is the BRIGHTEST star in the sky

When it comes to science, most grown-ups are very easily confused. It's no surprise that this is another thing they get wrong all the time.

Polaris is the scientific name for the North Star, or Pole Star. It's called that because it's very close to the North Pole, which is very handy if you happen to be lost on a starry night without a compass. It's the brightest star in the constellation Ursa Minor, but it's definitely not the brightest star in the sky. The brightest star is Sirius, which is much brighter than Polaris. In fact, Polaris isn't in the top ten brightest stars, or even the top twenty. So your grown-up is very wrong indeed.

Try it yourself...

... and see it isn't true.

★ To find Sirius, the brightest star in the sky, look for the constellation of Orion (this is best done during winter in the northern hemisphere). Follow the three stars of Orion's belt to the southeast.

★ To find the North Star, first find the Plough, or Big Dipper (which is part of the constellation Ursa Major). Follow the two stars that make up the edge of the Plough furthest away from the handle (one edge of the 'dipper') and the first star you come to is the North Star – this is the brightest star in the constellation Ursa Minor, also known as the Little Dipper (you can see why).

★ Compare the two. One of them is quite obviously brighter, isn't it?

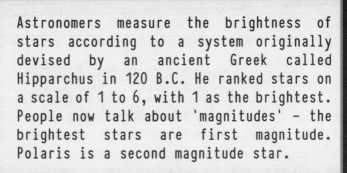

it's TRUE!

Astronomers measure the brightness of stars according to a system originally devised by an ancient Greek called Hipparchus in 120 B.C. He ranked stars on a scale of 1 to 6, with 1 as the brightest. People now talk about 'magnitudes' – the brightest stars are first magnitude. Polaris is a second magnitude star.

HEALTH 👁

Sitting too close to the television is BAD for your eyes

If you have parents, the chances are you'll have heard them say this.

Sitting too close to the telly isn't bad for your eyes, though it was until the late 1960s, when televisions used cathode-ray tubes. These emitted low levels of ultra violet radiation, and people were told not to sit closer than about two metres away from the TV screen. Now, it doesn't matter how close you sit.

On the other hand, sight problems are being liked to television, though not because of children sitting too close to them. Too much television can cause problems in focusing, especially in children under six years old.

> **it's TRUE!** The longest-running children's telly programme ever is Blue Peter. It's been on air since 1958.

FOOD AND DRINK 🥣

SUGAR makes children hyperactive

Many parents are sure this is true. Or could it be just another way of adults trying to spoil your fun?

Researchers have carried out various studies and none has found any evidence that sugar makes children hyperactive. In some studies, parents were told their children had eaten sweets when they hadn't, and that the children hadn't eaten sweets when they had. The parents thought the children were more out of control when they thought they'd been given sweets, not when they actually had eaten them. So it's all in adults' minds, and has nothing to do with reality.

SOME SWEET FACTS:

* The world's most popular chocolate bar is Snickers, which has been made since 1930.

* The most expensive chocolate in the world is made by Fritz Knipschildt in Connecticut, USA. His 'Madeleine' chocolates must be ordered in advance: each one, weighing about 40 grammes, costs US $250.

HUMAN BODY 🖐

Most of the body's HEAT is lost through the head

The chances are you'll have heard this from an adult as they try and force a woolly hat on your head. Next time, you'll be able to tell them it isn't true.

In fact, you don't lose any more heat from your head than any other part of your body of a similar size. Grown-ups are confused, it seems, because of a US army manual that made this claim in 1970 – it said that 40-45% of body heat is lost from the head. If that were true, not wearing a hat would make you just as cold as not wearing anything at all on your bottom half – try it yourself and see what you think.

> The phrase 'as mad as a hatter' probably comes from the use of mercury in the hat-making process. It's now known that mercury is toxic and contact with it can lead to severe nerve damage.

it's TRUE!

FOOD AND DRINK

Putting a teaspoon in the neck of a FIZZY-drink bottle helps the drink keep its fizz

Sometimes grown-ups like to perform little rituals to make them feel as though they have some control over things. Ask your grown-up why this works — they won't be able to tell you, mainly because it doesn't.

it's TRUE!

* Scientist Joseph Priestly invented the first man-made fizzy drinks (as opposed to naturally occurring fizzy water) in the late 1700s.

* The world's best known fizzy drink is Coca Cola, which was first made at the end of the 19th century and was intended as a medicine.

Try it yourself

... and find out it doesn't work

* Take two bottles of cola and pour a glass from each of them.

* Drink one glass while a friend drinks the other.

* Put a teaspoon in the neck of one bottle but leave the other one as it is.

* Leave the bottles alone for a couple of hours.

* Pour another glass from each bottle.

* Discover that there is no difference between them.

INVENTIONS AND DISCOVERIES

Alexander Fleming first DISCOVERED penicillin

Alexander Fleming did discover penicillin, but he wasn't the first, so your grown-up is wrong again.

Arabic tribesmen in North Africa had been using mould on damp saddles to treat saddle sores for hundreds of years. In the late 1890s, Arab stable hands at an army hospital in France were doing the same thing when a young doctor called Ernest Duchesne saw what they were doing, asked them about it and carried out his own experiments. His research was ignored, probably because he was only 23 and not a famous scientist, and Duchesne died in 1912.

Fleming was given a NOBEL PRIZE for his work in 1945

Alexander Fleming discovered penicillin in 1929 when he noticed some mould in his messy laboratory had killed off the bacteria he was studying. Fleming conducted his own experiments but eventually gave up the study of penicillin, which he named. Two chemists, Ernst Chain and Howard Florey, worked out how to purify and mass-produce penicillin. Fleming was given a Nobel Prize for his work in 1945, and in 1949 Duchesne was honoured for his work – though by that time it was a bit late for him.

it's TRUE!

Alfred Nobel, the inventor of dynamite, left money in his will to found the Nobel Prize, awarded every year since 1901 for achievements in physics, chemistry, medicine, literature and work for peace. So far 789 individuals have been awarded Nobel prizes, only 35 of them women.

FOOD AND DRINK 🥣

Margarine contains LESS fat than butter

Your grown-up will be enlightened when you tell them that butter and margarine both contain the same amount of fat.

The difference between butter and margarine is that the fat in butter is made up of more saturated fat. People who eat a lot of saturated fat tend to suffer from more heart attacks and strokes. We all need to eat fat as part of a healthy diet, but it's better to get it from vegetable oils, oily fish (like mackerel, sardines and salmon), nuts and seeds than from dairy products, meat, crisps and chocolate.

BUTTER is made up of more SATURATED FAT

FOODS HIGH IN SATURATED FAT

Don't eat too much of these...

Butter, ghee and lard

Coconut oil and palm oil

Sausages, meat pies and fatty meat

Cheese and cream

Ice cream

Chocolate

Cakes and biscuits

Crisps

Health 👁

Feed a cold and starve a FEVER

So goes an old saying, which a grown-up might tell you as they withhold your ice cream when you've a high temperature. Luckily, you can tell them they're talking rubbish again.

It's not a good idea either to eat a lot when you don't feel like it, or not to eat when you do feel like it, whether you've a fever, a cold, a broken wrist or a nosebleed. It might be that, in days gone by, people used to think that having a high temperature would be 'fuelled' by eating, so it was better not to eat, while having a 'chill' required feeding. Another theory goes that the original saying was 'feed a cold and stave a fever' – that is, if you eat a lot when you have a cold, it stops you from getting a fever. Whatever the origin of the saying, it's not true. If you're not well and you feel like eating, eat (whether you've a fever or not). If you don't feel like eating, don't. A few days without food won't kill you. The most important thing is to drink lots – more than you would normally.

HUMAN BODY
TEMPERATURES

* Normal body temperature, taken by placing a thermometer under the tongue, is **37 °C**, give or take half a degree or so.

* One or two degrees below this and the symptoms of hypothermia appear – this person needs medical treatment quickly.

* If someone's body temperature is above **38.5 °C** they should see a doctor. If the temperature is above **40 °C**, they need emergency medical treatment.

ANIMALS 🐤

If you HANDLE a baby bird it will be rejected by its parents

Grown-ups might tell you this because they don't want you to go near baby birds – and they might say the same thing about birds' eggs – or they might believe it's true. It isn't.

Most birds don't have a well-developed sense of smell, so unless they saw you handling a chick or egg they wouldn't know it had been handled by a human. But if you see a baby bird on the ground, hopping about looking confused, it doesn't necessarily mean that it's in trouble or abandoned. Lots of birds spend a few days on the ground while they're learning to fly. The best thing to do is to leave it alone – its parents will probably come for it. Generally, it's not a good idea to handle baby birds, but featherless babies aren't ready to learn to fly and have probably fallen from the nest, so it is better to replace them inside the nest. If in doubt, phone a vet or the RSPB.

So, while grown-ups are not telling the truth about birds being rejected by their parents due to human scent, they are right that it's not usually a good idea to touch them. You could tell them this to make them feel better.

FLIGHTLESS BIRDS

Some baby birds never learn to fly. These are the world's only surviving flightless birds:

* = two species
** = three species

⊛ = several species, some of which are
probably or almost flightless

FOOD AND DRINK 🥣

Coffee STUNTS your growth

Grown-ups agree on certain things: they do want you to eat broccoli, they do not want you to drink coffee. They might tell you that broccoli will give you all sorts of benefits (some of which are certainly true), while coffee is an evil substance that stops you from growing.

There's no research that proves coffee stunts your growth at all. On the other hand, coffee does contain caffeine, which isn't good for you. It can increase your heart rate, stop you from sleeping and make you feel irritable. Don't forget that some fizzy soft drinks contain caffeine too.

iT'S TRUE!

The world's most expensive coffee is called luak coffee. It's made from coffee beans that have been eaten by a wild cat called a luak, then partially digested and collected by people with one of the worst jobs in the world.

INVENTIONS AND DISCOVERIES

The GUILLOTINE was invented in France

Since guillotines were used to chop off so many people's heads during the French Revolution, it's not surprising that many adults believe this to be true. But of course it isn't.

The name 'guillotine' comes from a French doctor called Joseph Ignace Guillotin, who suggested a more humane method of execution for all criminals, rather than the previous methods of hanging the poor (which could take a long time) or beheading the rich. He put forward the idea of using a mechanical chopping machine, and Dr Antoine Louis had the first one built in 1792. But the guillotine, as it came to be known, wasn't the first mechanical head chopper – that was called the Halifax Gibbet, made in Yorkshire, England, in 1286 and used until 1650. The guillotine wasn't a new invention.

the guillotine wasn't the first MECHANICAL head chopper

it's TRUE!

Adults might also try and tell you that Dr Guillotin was executed during the French Revolution by guillotine. He wasn't - he died of an infection in 1814.

HEALTH 👁

Eating SPICY foods can give you an ulcer

When adults say this, they're usually referring to the kind of ulcer you get in your stomach or intestines, known as a peptic ulcer. But of course they are talking rubbish again.

Eating spicy food can't give you an ulcer, though it might irritate one you already have. Your adult might be confused because, in the past, doctors believed ulcers were caused by stress and spicy foods. But it's now known that the major cause of ulcers is a particular bacterium, and also certain kinds of pain killer. Ulcers have nothing to do with spices.

---

it's TRUE!

The Naga Jolokia is the world's hottest chilli pepper, according to the Guinness Book of World Records. It comes from north-eastern India and is named after the King Cobra (naga means King Cobra in the Indian language Sanskrit).

light bulb

Many adults are convinced of this but once again they are wrong.

An English physicist called Joseph Swan invented the light bulb in 1878, beating Thomas Edison to it. However, Edison did come up with some improvements to the light bulb: the first ones, invented by Swan, would only shine for a few seconds. Later, the two inventors formed a company together, called Ediswan.

It's TRUE!

The longest-burning light bulb is the Livermore light bulb, which has been burning since 1901 in a fire station in Livermore, California. It's only ever been switched off a few times, for a few days, to be moved to new sites.

Thomas Edison did invent lots of things and made vast improvements to others. He was very good at taking something that had already been invented and improving it so much that it could be used practically – as well as electric light, Edison also improved the telephone. His other really famous invention was the phonograph, a sort of early record player (which was a sort of early mp3 player...).

Edison did come up with some IMPROVEMENTS to the LIGHT bulb

SCIENCE

Some swimming pools contain a dye that turns WEE purple

Why on earth would an adult tell you this? To stop you from weeing in swimming pools, maybe?

There is no dye that can react to urine in a swimming pool and turn the area around the perpetrator into a billowing purple (or bright red or whatever colour your adult chooses) cloud. Who knows whether this particular lie is responsible for less wee in pools, or more – there are plenty of kids who would think it hilarious to have their wee turn purple in the pool. And who knows whether adults believe it themselves – let's hope so, because it would certainly stop them from weeing in pools. Whether you reveal the truth or not is up to you.

NO ONE SAID IT WOULDN'T TURN THE WATER YELLOW THOUGH!

There is **NO** dye that can react to urine in a swimming POOL

it's TRUE!

Water is a good breeding ground for harmful bacteria, so swimming pools have to be treated with chemicals to kill them off. The most popular swimming pool disinfectant is chlorine, which is added to the water as a chemical compound, which might be a solid, liquid or (more rarely) a gas.

Bonkers! ⊚

Eggs can be balanced on end on the day of the spring EQUINOX

To be fair, this is not one of the lies that grown-ups tell you. It's quite true that eggs can be balanced on end at the spring equinox, in the middle of March. What they forget to say is that eggs can be balanced on end on every other day of the year as well.

Spring time has lots of traditions involving eggs, which are a symbol of birth and fertility. Some of them, like egg decorating and, especially, eating chocolate eggs, are a lot of fun.

> **it's TRUE!**
>
> Only one type of mammal lays eggs: monotremes, which include four species of echidna and the duck-billed platypus. The duck-billed platypus is also unusual because it's one of a very few venomous mammals - it has a spur on its hind leg that delivers a powerful toxin.

ANIMALS 🐔

COCKROACHES would be the sole survivors of a nuclear apocalypse

It's true that they'd last longer than us, but they're not the hardest thing on the planet.

Cockroaches have been around for millions of years and are an awful lot tougher than us (see the fact box). Although they'd last longer than us in the event of a nuclear apocalypse, they wouldn't last as long as some other insects, such as fruit

BOOM!

AT LAST! THE WORLD IS OURS!

flies. Not many people like cockroaches, which scuttle about spreading disease and are very difficult to kill – so difficult that they've become famous as the sole survivors of a nuclear holocaust. In fact, if everything else died the only creatures left would probably be bacteria, which can live just about anywhere.

FIVE COCKROACH FACTS:

1. There are more than 5,000 species of cockroach.

2. Cockroaches have white blood.

3. Cockroaches can run at about 5.5 km/h – roughly human walking speed.

4. Cockroaches are found everywhere in the world except the Arctic and Antarctic.

5. Cockroaches really can live for a week without their heads.

FOOD AND DRINK 🥣

Fortune COOKIES come from China

Fortune cookies are those little biscuits you are given at the end of a Chinese meal. Break them open and find a 'fortune' on a piece of paper inside – it might be something like 'The one you love is closer than you think' or 'The more you give, the more you receive'. And, as any adult will tell you, they're Chinese. Except they're not.

Fortune cookies were probably invented by Chinese people living in California. Two Chinese people claiming to be the inventor came from San Francisco and Los Angeles. Others claim the cookies were copied from a Japanese tradition. Whatever their true origins, fortune cookies were definitely being given to diners in Chinese restaurants in California from the middle of the twentieth century, and from there spread to the rest of the United States and to the rest of the world – including China. In China they were unknown until the late 1980s, when they began to be imported from America.

Fortune cookies spread from CALIFORNIA to the rest of the US and to the rest of the WORLD - including China

it's TRUE!

An adult might tell you that chop suey was invented in America. They're wrong again - it is originally from the Chinese district of Taishan.

SCIENCE ✳

Plants take OXYGEN from the air at night so you shouldn't keep them in your bedroom

It's surprising how many adults still believe scientific thinking that was current in the middle of the 19th century.

Potted house plants were often removed from bedrooms in the 1800s because people believed the plants used up oxygen at night. Plants do use a small amount of oxygen at night, but during the day they more than make up for it by giving off oxygen and using up the carbon dioxide we breathe out. The tiny amount of oxygen a plant uses at night is nothing compared to the amount a sleeping person would use, proving that plants are much healthier than sleepovers.

> **it's TRUE!**
>
> There is one plant you definitely wouldn't want to grow in your bedroom. The Titam Arum, or corpse flower, smells like a rotting carcass to attract flies.

FOOD AND DRINK

Sushi is RAW fish

Many grown-ups are pretty ignorant about foreign food, and this is one of the many things they get wrong.

The word 'sushi' refers specifically to the rice eaten with other foods, but it can also mean the whole dish, including the rice plus pressed seaweed (nori), horseradish paste (wasabi), seafood (raw or cooked) and/or eggs or vegetables that go with it. If you want to refer to the raw fish on its own, the Japanese word is sashimi.

the JAPANESE word for raw fish is sashimi

UNUSUAL DISHES FROM AROUND THE WORLD

✱ Bird's nest soup is made from the nest of a particular kind of swift, which makes its nest out of saliva.

✱ Japanese fugu can be fatal if it isn't prepared correctly. Fugu, or pufferfish, contain a powerful poison that has to be expertly cut from the fish. Fugu chefs have to train for years.

✱ On the Indonesian island of Bali, deep-fried dragonflies are a popular appetizer.

✱ Hakarl is an Icelandic dish made from basking shark which has been buried for several months then hung up to dry.

HEALTH 👁

You SHOULDN'T swim (or even have a bath) within an hour of eating

Lots of grown-ups will try and stop you from swimming for an hour if you have so much as an apple. And some of them won't even let you have a bath. They are talking nonsense again.

Your misguided adult probably believes that if you do swim within an hour of eating, you could get stomach cramps and drown. However, there are no records of anyone drowning because they had eaten too recently. If you'd just had a five-course dinner then immediately launched yourself into a lake for a two-kilometre swim, you might find you got tired and into trouble before you reached the other side. But you probably wouldn't feel like a really long swim at the end of a huge meal. Perhaps your adult thinks that you're more likely to get cramp in your limbs when exercising after a meal, because your body is busy digesting the food – there might be some truth in this, but if you do get cramp while swimming (and this is quite common anyway), you just need to float for a while and wait for the cramp to go away. As for waiting an hour before having a bath – that's just bonkers.

there are **NO** RECORDS of anyone drowning because they had EATEN too recently

it's TRUE!

The longest swim ever recorded was from Mexico to Cuba, a distance of 197 km, swum by Australian Susie Maroney in 1998.

INVENTIONS AND DISCOVERIES

Henry Ford built the world's first motor CAR

Your adult has become confused once again. Henry Ford did build motor cars, and he built them a long time ago, but he wasn't the first person to do so.

Henry Ford is most famous for the Model T, a passenger car that was revolutionary because it was affordable by ordinary people and not only the very rich. He sold 15.5 million of the cars in the United States, where he had his factory. He's also famous for introducing factory assembly lines, which meant his cars could be made quickly and efficiently.

But Ford didn't build the first ever motor car. In 1771 Nicolas Joseph Cugnot designed a steam-powered, three-wheeled car, but it was slower, more dangerous and more difficult to operate than a horse pulling a carriage. A more practical car was powered by a gasoline engine – Gottleib Daimler built the first one in 1895, and the following year Karl Benz received the first patent for a gas-fuelled car.

It's TRUE!

The fastest car in the world is currently the SSC Ultimate Aero, with a top speed of 414 km/h. If you want to buy one, you'll need US $654,400.

He's also **FAMOUS** for introducing FACTORY ASSEMBLY lines, which meant his cars could be made **quickly** and **EFFICIENTLY**

BONKERS! 🌀

You should wee on a JELLYFISH sting to neutralize it

Apart from being very unpleasant indeed, do grown-ups really think that weeing on a wound is a good idea? Strange though it may seem, some of them do.

Many jellyfish stings can be relieved by applying something acidic, such as vinegar, or baking powder mixed with sea water. Human wee is sometimes acidic, but not always – it depends what the wee-er has been drinking and eating. If

I'M STINGING IN THE RAIN!

you rinse the jellyfish stings with fresh water it can make the stingers release more venom, so the victim will be in even more pain (and the same thing can happen if the person doing the weeing has been drinking a lot of water). Rinsing with sea water is a much better, and far less revolting, idea.

It's TRUE!

Jellyfish stings aren't usually life threatening. But the sea creature responsible for the most human deaths is the box jellyfish (which isn't really a jellyfish but a cubazoa). It's one of the most venomous animals in the world: its venom can kill a human in three minutes.

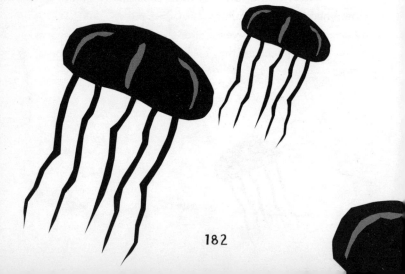

SCIENCE

NEANDERTHALS were stupid sub-humans

The Neanderthals are badly misunderstood by many grown-ups. Either they think Neanderthals were half-witted, grunting sub-humans, or they think we evolved from them. Either way, they're talking rubbish again.

Neanderthals were a human-like species that was around at the same time as modern humans and our ancestors. Far from being stupid, they had brains almost the same size as our own, and there's evidence that they cared for their sick, buried their dead and had their own culture. They died out around 28,000 years ago, around 10,000 years after the first modern humans appeared, perhaps because they couldn't compete with our own ancestors.

The latest **GENETIC** evidence suggests that our ANCESTORS interbred with Neanderthals – so (although we didn't evolve from them) there's a little bit of Neanderthal in all of US

it's TRUE!

Scientists used to think that Neanderthals couldn't speak. In 1983 a Neanderthal bone was discovered that proved them wrong – the bone was almost exactly the same as the hyoid bone in humans, which forms part of the vocal mechanism.

OUT NOW➔

BONKERS BOOKS

why HEADLESS CHICKENS run

and OTHER BONKERS things you need to KNOW

YOU ARE FEELING SLEEPY!

NO I'M NOT.

you can HYPNOTIZE an alligator

MICHAEL COX

The CAT-MIAOW machine

This mechanical cat was invented in Japan in 1963 to scare off mice and rats. It meowed ten times a minute and the eyes lit up each time it did (but it was later beaten to death by a gang of mechanical rats).

The completely circular BATTLE ship

Named the 'POPOVKA' after Admiral Popov, the Russian who designed it in 1873. Despite having its six enormous engines going at full speed, the 'POPOVKA' could only travel at 6 mph. This was slower than the current of the river on which these saucer-shaped ships were tested, so not only were they instantly swept out to sea, but they twizzled around and around, making their sailors really sea-sick. When the crew tried to fire the guns, their recoil also caused the ship to rotate, so the guns were no longer pointing at the target. Now you know why you see so few circular ships.

TEN TOTALLY BONKERS FIRST NAMES

All used between 1838 and 1900

Abisha

Babberley

Strongitharm

Tram

Murder

Brained

Lettuce

Bugless

Dozer

Despair

Each year in Britain approximately...

700 children get marbles stuck up their noses.

16,000 people are injured by the cushions known as pouffes.

2,000 people are injured trying to open tins of corned beef.

1,500 people have hospital treatment for accidents involving tissue paper.

37,000 people are treated for accidents involving slippers.

WHY DO WE SAY ... IT'S RAINING CATS AND DOGS?

We usually only say this when it's raining really, really heavily. In other words, when we're suffering the sort of torrential downpours which, more often than not lead to flooding. Nowadays, we're fortunate enough to have things like man-made gutters, soakaways, drains and river embankments, which lessen the effects of these heavy rainstorms. However, in times-gone-by, cities, towns and villages had no such things. So when it rained really heavily, lanes and alleyways were soon were soon waist-deep with swirling flood waters which swept away everyone and everything in their path. Another thing these places didn't have were sanctuaries for abandoned dogs and cats and as a result the streets were always full of forlorn Fidos and forsaken Felixes. So when it rained really heavily, lots and lots of these stray pets would be caught up in the surging floodwater and drowned. Consequently people would soon be seeing the bodies of the unfortunate creatures floating past, or even through, their houses. 'Well!' they'd exclaim, 'Would you look at that. It's raining cat and dogs!' (and after the storm the streets would be full of poodles).